CW01301733

Expanding Classics

This volume explores innovative ways of expanding classical languages and cultures to educational and museum audiences.

It shows that classical subjects have an important role to play within society and can enrich individuals' lives in many different, and perhaps surprising, ways. Chapters present projects covering literacy and engagement with reading, empowering students to understand and use new types of vocabulary, discovering the personal relevance of ancient history and the resonance of ancient material culture and stories. Contributors demonstrate that classical subjects can be taught cost-effectively and inclusively by non-specialist teachers and in non-traditional settings. In their various ways, they highlight the need to rethink the role of Classics in twenty-first-century classrooms and communities. Recommendations are made for further development, including ways to improve research, policy and practice in the field of Classics education.

Expanding Classics presents an important series of case studies on classical learning, of interest to museum educators, teacher trainers, school leaders and curriculum designers, as well as those teaching in primary, secondary and further education settings in the UK and worldwide.

Arlene Holmes-Henderson is an Associate Professor of Classics and Ancient History at Durham University. She works at the intersection of research, policy and practice to improve access to the study of classical subjects in schools and communities in the UK and worldwide. She teaches in the School of Education and leads several research projects exploring the role of Classics in the curriculum.

Classics In and Out of the Academy
Classical Pedagogy in the Twenty-First Century
Series editors – Fiona McHardy and Nancy Rabinowitz

This series of short volumes explores the ways in which the study of antiquity can enrich the lives of diverse populations in the twenty-first century. The series covers two distinct, but interrelated topics: 1) ways in which classicists can engage new audiences within the profession by embedding inclusivity and diversity in school and university teaching practices, curricula, and assessments, and 2) the relevance of Classics to learners from the most marginalized social strata (e.g. the incarcerated, refugees, those suffering from mental illness).

Classics and Prison Education in the US
Edited by Emilio Capettini and Nancy Sorkin Rabinowitz

Classics at Primary School
A Tool for Social Justice
Evelien Bracke

Expanding Classics
Practitioner Perspectives from Museums and Schools

Edited by
Arlene Holmes-Henderson

Routledge
Taylor & Francis Group
LONDON AND NEW YORK

First published 2023
by Routledge
4 Park Square, Milton Park, Abingdon, Oxon OX14 4RN

and by Routledge
605 Third Avenue, New York, NY 10158

Routledge is an imprint of the Taylor & Francis Group, an informa business

© 2023 selection and editorial matter, Arlene Holmes-Henderson; individual chapters, the contributors

The right of Arlene Holmes-Henderson to be identified as the author of the editorial material, and of the authors for their individual chapters, has been asserted in accordance with sections 77 and 78 of the Copyright, Designs and Patents Act 1988.

All rights reserved. No part of this book may be reprinted or reproduced or utilised in any form or by any electronic, mechanical, or other means, now known or hereafter invented, including photocopying and recording, or in any information storage or retrieval system, without permission in writing from the publishers.

Trademark notice: Product or corporate names may be trademarks or registered trademarks, and are used only for identification and explanation without intent to infringe.

British Library Cataloguing-in-Publication Data
A catalogue record for this book is available from the British Library

Library of Congress Cataloging-in-Publication Data
Names: Holmes-Henderson, Arlene, editor.
Title: Inclusive classics : innovative pedagogies in museums and schools /Arlene Holmes-Henderson.
Description: First Edition. | New York : Routledge, 2023. | Series: Classics in and out of the academy: Classical pedagogy in the twenty-first century | Includes bibliographical references and index. |
Identifiers: LCCN 2022043450 (print) | LCCN 2022043451 (ebook) | ISBN 9781032021140 (Hardback) | ISBN 9781032021171 (Paperback) | ISBN 9781003181958 (eBook)
Subjects: LCSH: Classical education--Great Britain. | Multicultural education--Great Britain--Case studies. | Multilingual education--Great Britain--Case studies. | Anthropological museums and collections--Great Britain. | Education--Great Britain--History.
Classification: LCC LC1011 .I53 2023 (print) | LCC LC1011 (ebook) | DDC 370.1170941--dc23/eng/20220928
LC record available at https://lccn.loc.gov/2022043450
LC ebook record available at https://lccn.loc.gov/2022043451

ISBN: 978-1-032-02114-0 (hbk)
ISBN: 978-1-032-02117-1 (pbk)
ISBN: 978-1-003-18195-8 (ebk)

DOI: 10.4324/9781003181958

Typeset in Times New Roman
by KnowledgeWorks Global Ltd.

For Dr Emily Helene Matters 1946–2021
sic itur ad astra
(Virgil, Aeneid IX, 641)

Contents

List of Figures and Map ix
List of Tables x
List of Contributors xi
Acknowledgements xiii
List of Abbreviations xiv

Introduction 1
ARLENE HOLMES-HENDERSON

1 **Ancient languages for 6- to 11-year-olds: Exploring three pedagogical approaches via a longitudinal study** 8
ARLENE HOLMES-HENDERSON

2 **Including the excluded: Teaching Latin in an area of high socio-economic disadvantage** 30
PETER WRIGHT

3 **Using classical mythology to teach English as an Additional Language** 42
ANNA BLOOR, MEGHAN McCABE AND ARLENE HOLMES-HENDERSON

4 **Student perceptions of BAME people in the Roman world: A comparison of Latin textbooks** 56
ALEX GRUAR

5 **Promoting inclusivity through teaching Ancient History** 72
ANNA McOMISH

6 **Whose museum is it anyway? Connecting with communities at the Museum of Classical Archaeology, Cambridge** 90
SUSANNE TURNER

7 **Contested Collections: Using 3D replicas to present new narratives of objects with contested histories** 110
EMMA PAYNE AND LAURA GIBSON

Index 128

Figures and Map

Figures

1.1	Progress by all pupils.	12
1.2	Progress of pupils by duration (years) of attending The Latin Programme.	13
1.3	Progress of FSM-eligible and non-FSM-eligible pupils.	14
1.4	Progress of pupils with SEN and No SEN pupils.	16
1.5	Progress of pupils with EAL and pupils with L1 English.	17
1.6	End of workshop teacher responses regarding introducing Latin.	23
1.7	End of workshop teacher responses regarding introducing Ancient Greek.	23
5.1	This figure illustrates how including study of the Ancient Middle East in the KS3 curriculum supported students' learning in their subsequent GCSE topic on the Persian Empire, creating a spiral curriculum that established beneficial schemata.	76
6.1	Mentimeter presentation slide. The results of a poll exercise during a session with young people.	103
6.2	Mentimeter presentation slide. The feedback received after a session with young people.	103
7.1	Contested Collections logo.	111
7.2	Excerpt from the Parthenon Sculptures object narrative.	113
7.3	Excerpt from the Gweagal Shield object narrative showing a student 'Thinking Point'.	118
7.4	(a-c) Handling three of the Contested Collection objects: the metope from the Parthenon, a Benin Bronze plaque and the Hoa Hakananai'a.	119

Map

2.1	Locations of educational institutions providing Latin teaching in Blackpool and the surrounding area.	32

Tables

4.1	Pupil responses to the first survey question: Are there any BAME characters in your Latin course book? This question refers to your Suburani textbook/Activebook if you are in Year Eight, and the Cambridge Latin Course Book 1/web book if you are in Year Nine	65
4.2	Pupil responses to the second survey question: How many Black, Asian or minority ethnic (BAME) people do you think there were in Roman society?	65
4.3	Pupil responses to the third survey question: If you answered yes, how do you think BAME characters are portrayed in the book?	66
5.1	The KS3 History curriculum at Aldridge School with changes from summer 2019 in bold	74
5.2	Ancient Middle East 3000-479 BCE: enquiry questions and lesson order	78
7.1	The eight shortlisted objects selected by the King's College London students	122

Contributors

Anna Bloor teaches English to students aged 11–18 at The Bemrose School, Derby, England. She is interested in female perspectives in literature and the impact of oracy on extended writing. As a teacher of children with English as an Additional Language, she is passionate about making reading an engaging activity for all.

Laura Gibson is a Lecturer in the Department of Digital Humanities at King's College London, England. Her research on decolonisation and digitisation is informed by several years of working in South African museums. Laura's current research considers issues of indigenous knowledge exchange and repatriation from colonial institutions using digital tools.

Alex Gruar is a teacher of Classics at Aylesbury Grammar School, England. Prior to this, she taught in both independent and state-maintained schools, as well as OxLAT, a University of Oxford programme to extend GCSE Latin to those who would not otherwise have access to the subject.

Arlene Holmes-Henderson is an Associate Professor of Classics and Ancient History at Durham University, England. She works at the intersection of research, policy and practice to improve access to the study of classical subjects in schools and communities in the UK and worldwide.

Meghan McCabe is the Head of Sixth Form and a teacher of English at The Bemrose School in Derby, England, and has an MA in Educational Leadership. She is interested in curriculum design and making classical texts accessible to the large group of children with English as an Additional Language who attend the school.

xii *Contributors*

Anna McOmish is the Head of History at Aldridge School, England; OCR examiner for Ancient History GCSE; and a convert to the world of Classics. She has an MA in Teaching Studies from the University of Birmingham and is especially interested in the inclusion and impact of diverse history at Key Stage Three.

Emma Payne is a Visiting Research Fellow in the Classics Department, King's College London, England. Trained as a conservator, her research examines object materiality, particularly ancient Greek and Roman sculpture. Her monograph, *Casting the Parthenon Sculptures from the Eighteenth Century to the Digital Age*, was published in April 2021.

Susanne Turner is the Curator of the Museum of Classical Archaeology at the University of Cambridge, England. She manages and administers the Museum, curates its collections, and develops the museum service in collaboration with the Museum Director, the Museum Education and Outreach Co-ordinator and the Museum and Collections Assistant.

Peter Wright has taught A-Level Ancient History and Classical Civilisation at Blackpool Sixth Form College, England, since 2006, and he coordinates the teaching of Latin and Classics in several local state-maintained schools. A Times Educational Supplement Further Education Teacher of the Year award winner, he is a Specialist Leader of Education for History.

Acknowledgements

My professional life has collaboration at its heart. This book is the product of numerous partnerships and joint activities with colleagues in museum and school contexts. Linking most of the chapters in this volume, in one way or another, is the Advocating Classics Education project. Funded by the Arts and Humanities Research Council in 2017, this project has been pivotal to the resurgence of Classics in communities around the UK. It is to my co-director, Professor Edith Hall, that I owe the greatest gratitude: her unfailing energy and commitment to widening access to the study of the ancient world have been inspirational.

I must also record special thanks to the contributors without whom this book would not have been possible. Many are practising teachers in primary and secondary schools who spent their evenings, weekends and school holidays (during the pandemic years 2020–2022) writing for publication in this volume. They represent the very best of their profession. The academic and museum-based contributors were equally committed to our shared goal; their innovative practice engages new audiences with ancient culture and deserves to be shared widely.

I have been fortunate to benefit from the wisdom and support of Professor Fiona McHardy and Professor Nancy Rabinowitz as series editors. Their patience, good humour and insightful feedback have made the draft-to-publication experience a pleasure. Excellent assistance has been available from the team at Routledge Classics, including Amy Davis-Poynter and Marcia Adams. But the person who has been at my side throughout the whole process is my research assistant Katrina Kelly. Her expertise and enthusiasm were the winning combination which kept morale high while preparing the manuscript for submission.

Arlene Holmes-Henderson

Abbreviations

A-Level   The Advanced Level is a subject-based qualification conferred as part of the General Certificate of Education at a higher level than the GCSE and the O Level. It is an examination taken by students aged 17–18 in secondary education in England, Wales and Northern Ireland. A-Levels are usually treated as a measure of attainment suitable for university entry.
ACE   Advocating Classics Education.
AQA   The Assessment and Qualifications Alliance.
AS Level   Advanced Subsidiary Level – the AS Level is a subject-based qualification taken at the midpoint of the two-year course of study which the A-Level comprises. Students may complete their studies at the end of the AS Level or use it to complete their qualification at the higher A-Level standard.
BAME   Black, Asian and minority ethnic.
BLM   Black Lives Matter.
CCA   Cambridge Community Arts.
CPD   Continuing Professional Development.
CSCP   The Cambridge School Classics Project.
EAL   English as an Additional Language.
FE   Further Education includes any study after secondary education that is not part of higher education (that is, not taken as part of an undergraduate or graduate degree).
FSM   Free School Meals.
GCSE   The General Certificate of Secondary Education is an academic qualification awarded in a specified subject to students aged 14–16 in secondary education in England, Wales and Northern Ireland.
GRT   Gypsy, Roma and Traveller Community.

Abbreviations xv

IMD	Index of Multiple Deprivation. The official measure of deprivation for areas of England.
ITE	Initial Teacher Education.

Key Stages are the official terms for the periods of schooling in maintained schools in England and Wales.

KS1	Key Stage One refers to the period of two years comprising Years One and Two (preceded by Reception) when students are aged 5–7.
KS2	Key Stage Two refers to the period of four years comprising Years Three, Four, Five and Six when students are aged 7–11.
KS3	Key Stage Three refers to the period of three years comprising Years Seven, Eight and Nine when students are aged 12–14.
KS4	Key Stage Four refers to the period of two years which incorporate GCSEs, and other examinations, during Year 10 and Year 11, when students are aged 14–16.
KS5	Key Stage Five refers to the period of two years of education comprising Years 12–13 when students are aged 16–18.
MFL	Modern Foreign Language.
MOCA	The Museum of Classical Archaeology at the University of Cambridge.
NPO	National Portfolio Organisation.
OCR	Oxford, Cambridge and RSA Examinations.
Ofsted	The Office for Standards in Education, Children's Services and Skills is a non-ministerial department of the UK government. The services Ofsted inspects or regulates include: state-maintained schools, independent schools and teacher training providers, colleges, and learning and skills providers in England.
PGCE	Postgraduate Certificate in Education. A one-year higher education course in England, Wales and Northern Ireland which trains graduates to become teachers.
PP	Pupil Premium. Funding granted to schools to improve educational outcomes for disadvantaged pupils.
PRU	Pupil Referral Unit. An educational setting which caters for children who are unable to attend mainstream school for a range of reasons, such as illness or exclusion.

xvi *Abbreviations*

SATs	Standard Assessment Tests. These measure student achievement in Maths and Reading at the end of **Key Stage One** and the end of **Key Stage Two** in English schools.
SCITT	School-Centred Initial Teacher Training.
SEN(D)	Special Educational Needs (and Disability).
Year Seven	The first year of **KS3** when students are aged 11–12.
Year Eight	The second year of **KS3** when students are aged 12–13.
Year Nine	The third year of **KS3** when students are aged 13–14.
Year Ten	The first year of **KS4** when students are aged 14–15.
Year 11	The second year of **KS4** when students are aged 15–16.
Year 12	The first year of **KS5** when students are aged 16–17.
Year 13	The second year of **KS5** when students are aged 17–18.

Table 1 The education system in England and Wales

		England and Wales		
Age	Year group	Key Stage	Type of school	
4	Reception	Foundation	Primary	Infants
5	Y1	KS1		
6	Y2			
7	Y3	KS2		Juniors
8	Y4			
9	Y5			
10	Y6			
11	Y7	KS3	Secondary	Secondary/ High School/ Community College
12	Y8			
13	Y9			
14	Y10	KS4		
15	Y11			
16	Y12	KS5	Non-Compulsory/ Further Education	Lower Sixth
17	Y13			Upper Sixth
18				

Introduction

Arlene Holmes-Henderson

This volume brings together schoolteachers, academics and museum educators to share practice-based research from a range of learning contexts. It paints a picture of innovation both within and outside the classroom, showcasing multiple perspectives from practitioners whose work is expanding Classics to engage new audiences. Contributors present case studies from across England, including primary schools in London and Oxford and a pupil referral unit, sixth form college and schools across Lancashire in the North West. Research conducted in secondary schools in the East and West Midlands and Buckinghamshire provide new insights into the learning and teaching of Latin, Classical Civilisation and Ancient History, and museum-focussed educational initiatives in London and Cambridge complete the collection.

Access to classical subjects in English schools currently relies on 'wealth or luck' (Hunt and Holmes-Henderson 2021). There is a startling disparity of access to classical subjects across regions of England, with schools in London and the South East being far more likely to offer Latin, Classical Greek, Classical Civilisation and Ancient History than schools in other parts of the country (Hunt and Holmes-Henderson 2021). The independent (fee-paying) sector dominates the teaching and learning of classical languages; in 2019, for example, a student was 'four times more likely to be able to enter A-Level Latin in an independent school than in a state-maintained school' (Hunt and Holmes-Henderson 2021). Yet 93 per cent of young people in England attend state-maintained schools (Ashton 2022).

Cunliffe (2022) warns that 'As long as Latin and Greek remain inaccessible, confined to the upper echelons, they'll retain their disproportionate power to dazzle and awe'. Edith Hall (2019) explains how, historically, a classical education in England was reserved for wealthy young men, whose studies of Latin and Greek provided them with a

DOI: 10.4324/9781003181958-1

'patina of gentlemanliness as well as access to Oxford and Cambridge'. Ancient languages were deemed a marker of intellect and status and were deployed as such, with knowledge utilised in places of power, from the lawcourts to the medical theatre, and the House of Commons. Cunliffe (2022) claims that the same is true today, 'An aspiring politician can deflect attention away from his personal inadequacies and glaring lack of ideology or integrity by peppering a speech with a few choice quotes from Pericles or Cicero'. Senior politicians such as Boris Johnson and Jacob Rees-Mogg have been criticised for employing classical references in political communications 'proclaiming themselves members of that elite, and hence—it is fair to infer—destined to rule the lower orders' (Campbell 2019). Using Classics to obfuscate, rather than clarify, meaning does little to reduce the elitist connotations of the discipline. This is especially the case since Johnson and Rees-Mogg attended one of England's leading independent boarding schools, where Classics has flourished on the curriculum for centuries. Headteachers of non-selective state-maintained schools are, understandably, often apprehensive about introducing Classics to their school curriculum. They ask, 'How compatible is the study of Classics with the young people in my school, many of whom experience barriers to their learning?'. This volume shares some emerging answers.

The relationship between classical subjects in the curriculum and social justice has received new attention from theoretical and policy-informed perspectives (Hunt 2018, Capettini and Rabinowitz 2021, Bracke 2022). Classical culture, white-washed and idealised, became the curriculum of empire and a blueprint for conquest and discrimination (Goff 2005; Bradley 2010; Agbamu 2019, 2021, 2022). Classics' complex and painful history of appropriation by far-right groups for justifying prejudice, social cleansing and exclusionary policies has left an indelible stain on the subject (Zuckerburg 2018). This forms part of the discipline's history which is rightly the focus of increasing research and critique. Although this critical evaluation of Classics as a discipline (and its 'reception') is not currently included in the examination syllabus for classical subjects in English schools, expansion to include it would certainly be valuable in future (it forms an important part of the curriculum in Denmark [Andersen et al. 2019]).

Classics undergraduate Janek Drevikovsky (2019), at the University of Sydney, suggests that we 'reflect on the ancient past, and how its knowledge and cultures can enrich our lives. School can help young people do this'. One encouraging trend from England is that Ancient History is currently seeing an increase in student numbers (age 14–18) and, at A-Level in 2019, was available in twice as many schools in the state-maintained sector than in the independent sector. The number of schools, though, is still low: 46 state-maintained (1.3 per cent of all state-maintained schools) compared to 20 independent schools (0.86 per cent of all independent schools [Hunt and Holmes-Henderson 2021]). Ancient History appears to be the qualification most available in the state-maintained sector but these statistics provide a sobering indication of the national picture.

This volume brings a critical, bottom-up and context-dependent approach to issues pertaining to Classics teaching and learning. In doing so, it does three things. Firstly, it fills the gap in cross-curricular manuals which provide examples of good practice in History and Languages but say nothing about Classics (Cole 2009). Secondly, it responds to the objections raised by Amor et al. (2019) and Oliver (2013) that academic and philosophical discussions of inclusive pedagogy centre on 'theory' and 'description' but lack a focus on engagement with the real world (Koutsoris et al. 2022). Thirdly, it expands the traditional remit of 'Classics' research to include interdisciplinary, practice-based research which is education-focussed.

Of course, this short collection does not claim to provide a comprehensive compendium of practices which expand access to Classics education. The book has grown from a series of events such as 'Towards a more Inclusive Classics I and II', 'The Classical Association annual conference pedagogy panels', 'TeachMeet English Icons', 'Team English National Conference', 'Academus Classics Outreach conference', 'Classics for All online TeachMeets' and 'Connecting Classical Collections network meetings'. Thus, the chapters presented here illuminate the professional practice of a small number of research-active contributors, most of whom have conducted this research in their own time. For the majority of the contributors, it is their first peer-reviewed publication. The activities associated with expanding Classics are showcased in this volume by a predominantly female team. Their circumstances reflect those of so many who are committed to widening access; time pressures, caring responsibilities (including parental leave), disability, working-class background, first generation university participation, precarious and/or part-time employment. These barriers affect marginalised voices within the Classics community disproportionately. A wider range of perspectives, particularly those from BAME, indigenous and LGBTQIA+ authors, would ensure better representation of the voices, opinions and experiences of those from communities under-represented in Classics academic publishing. They would also help educators at all levels make research-informed decisions about what to teach, and how. Our hope is that the initiatives described here will provide a launchpad for further research into the learning and teaching of classical subjects in museums, schools, further education colleges and in adult education environments.

In Chapter One, Arlene Holmes-Henderson, Associate Professor of Classics and Ancient History at Durham University and Principal Investigator of the Classics in Communities project, explores how Latin and Ancient Greek can be used to support English literacy development. Previously heralded as languages most suitable for study by children of high prior attainment, the so-called gifted and talented, research recently undertaken in schools demonstrates that it is children who are performing below age-related expectations who benefit most from learning Latin and Ancient Greek. This chapter provides quantitative and qualitative data from a five-year longitudinal educational study in areas of socio-economic disadvantage which illuminates the particular value of classical languages in closing the literacy attainment gap for children learning English as an additional language, children eligible for Free School Meals and children with Special Educational Needs. Several of these children would have been excluded from Latin classes just two decades ago, yet research now indicates that they are the ones who benefit most from exposure to an ancient language.

In Chapter Two, Peter Wright, a Specialist Leader of Education for History and an experienced teacher of A-Level Ancient History and Classical Civilisation at Blackpool Sixth Form College, investigates the impact of classical subjects upon groups who have not traditionally had access to Classics, in this case students from an area of chronic social and economic disadvantage. He charts the successful introduction and growth of Latin in colleges, schools and a Pupil Referral Unit in the local area. He suggests that incorporating Latin into the curriculum by training non-specialist teachers can be beneficial for both staff and students, resulting in significant and measurable improvements in vocabulary development for pupils who face multiple barriers to their learning and who might be labelled 'hardest to reach'.

Chapter Three highlights the impact of Classics in translation, specifically ancient mythology, to support and develop the teaching of English as an Additional Language to pupils at The Bemrose School in Derby. Anna Bloor and Meghan McCabe, both teachers in the English department at this non-selective state-maintained secondary school, share a passion for making reading engaging and for making classical texts accessible to pupils for whom English is not their first language. They bring perspectives and experience from curriculum design, oracy education and educational leadership to this chapter which showcases classical mythology as a catalyst for functional literacy, oral fluency and cultural literacy for newly arrived refugee students. *The Odyssey* was found to offer excellent opportunities for reading aloud, reciprocal reading, and developing additional skills in speaking, listening and writing, all of which contributed to pupils' improved confidence and proficiency in English.

Chapter Four captures the importance of textbook creators' choice of content, particularly characters, plot and illustrations, for students' perceptions of the ancient world. Alex Gruar, a teacher of Classics at Aylesbury Grammar School and former teacher of OxLAT, a University of Oxford programme to extend GCSE Latin to those who would not otherwise have access to the subject, undertook research to explore how teaching Latin via the *Cambridge Latin Course* and *Suburani* coursebooks impacted students' understanding of the prevalence and role of Black, Asian and minority ethnic people in the Roman world. This chapter encourages readers to expand access to, and definitions of, 'Classics' via teaching materials which represent diversity within, and beyond, the Roman world.

In Chapter Five, Anna McOmish, Head of History at Aldridge School in Walsall and an OCR examiner for Ancient History GCSE, explores the impact of teaching diverse history to pupils from a range of ethnic backgrounds at Key Stage Three as preparation for examination at GCSE and A-Level. She highlights how Islamic peoples or modern geographical regions with large Muslim populations are still under-represented at both Key Stage Three and GCSE level in school History curricula and textbooks. When Muslim students do find representation in the History curriculum, this can often be through a lens of the 'subjugated', and as one ethnic group of many vying for representation within a white-European dominated narrative. This chapter explores the impact of expanding the curriculum to include the study of the Ancient Middle East on the learning experiences of Muslim students at one school in the West Midlands. Impacts investigated were 'inclusion' and 'success' where success is measured in terms of academic attainment, knowledge retention, intellectual curiosity and subject engagement.

In Chapter Six, Susanne Turner, the Curator of the Museum of Classical Archaeology at the University of Cambridge, discusses how small museums with a limited budget can nevertheless have a big impact on local communities by engaging audiences who would not otherwise encounter classical subjects and who may traditionally have faced barriers of access to the Museum. She evaluates the role of museums in expanding access to Classics through a range of media and focuses upon recent projects at The Museum of Classical Archaeology, including *Drink and Draw*, *Queer Antiquities*, *Bridging*

Binaries, the *Minimus Primary Latin Project, Go Figure!* and *Beyond the Pale*. Reframing classical collections is an important practice and by offering opportunities to engage with, and reinterpret classical objects, the Museum also helps new audiences to foster a relationship with the ancient past.

In Chapter Seven, Emma Payne, a Conservator of Ancient Greek and Roman sculpture and Visiting Research Fellow in the Classics department at King's College London, and Laura Gibson, a researcher in indigenous knowledge exchange and repatriation from colonial institutions and a Lecturer in the Department of Digital Humanities at King's College London, discuss the *Contested Collections* project. This project aims to provide primary school learners with the skills, language and confidence to engage in complex debates around issues of restitution and decolonisation by providing sets of learning materials and new narratives concerning artefacts whose ownership, acquisition or histories are contested. Central to the project are high-quality 3D prints of the artefacts to encourage interactions not possible with the original works. Objects include those from the classical world, for example the Parthenon, and high-profile cases like the Benin Bronzes, but are not limited to ancient artefacts. This chapter examines the development of the project, its collaboration with a number of partners and close involvement of a diverse group of student volunteers, while looking towards its future delivery and impact on school learners.

These chapters highlight innovative practice-based research which has expanded Classics to new educational and museum audiences. In their various ways, they highlight the need to rethink the role of Classics in twenty-first century classrooms and communities, and include recommendations for further development, including research, policy and practice. While the examples showcased here are from the English education system, we hope that readers outside England will identify ideas which can be applied or adapted for use in other countries.

Reference List

Agbamu, S. 2019. "Mare Nostrum: Italy and the Mediterranean of Ancient Rome in the Twentieth and Twenty-First Centuries". *Fascism* 8 (2): 250–274.

Agbamu, S. 2021. "The Reception of Petrarch's *Africa* in Fascist Italy". *International Journal of the Classical Tradition* 29: 83–102.

Agbamu, S. 2022. "Classics and Italian colonialism: an outsider's perspective". *Italian Studies in South Africa* 35 (1): 29–32.

Amor, A. M., M. Hagiwara, K. A. Shogren, J. R. Thompson, M. A. Verdugo, K. M. Burke and V. Aguayo. 2019. "International perspectives and trends in research on inclusive education: A systematic review". *International Journal of Inclusive Education* 23 (12): 1277–1295.

Andersen, L. M., T. M. Kristensen and V. Nørskov. 2019. "Classical Antiquity in the Danish Classroom: "Oldtidskundskab" as Heritage". In Classical Heritage and European Identities: The Imagined Geographies of Danish Classicism, 19–43. London: Routledge.

Ashton, H. 2022. "Class Inequality in the Creative Industries is rooted in unequal access to arts and cultural education". *Policy and Evidence Centre Blog*. Accessed 10 June 2022. https://pec.ac.uk/blog/class-inequality-in-the-creative-industries-is-rooted-in-unequal-access-to-arts-and-cultural-education.

Bracke, E. 2022. *Classics in primary schools: a tool for social justice*. London: Routledge.

Bradley, M. 2010. *Classics and imperialism in the British Empire*. Oxford: Oxford University Press.

Campbell, G. 2019. "Why posh politicians pretend to speak Latin". *Oxford University Press Blog*, 10 June. Accessed 28 July 2022. https://blog.oup.com/2019/06/why-posh-politicians-pretend-speak-latin/.

Capettini, E. and N. S. Rabinowitz. 2021. Classics and Prison Education in the US. London: Routledge.

Cole, M. 2009. *Equality in the secondary school: promoting good practice across the curriculum*. London: Continuum.

Cunliffe, R. 2022. "Latin and Greek are not just for the elite". *The New Statesman*, 26 July. Accessed 28 July 2022. https://www.newstatesman.com/politics/education/2022/07/latin-greek-classics-elite.

Drevikovsky, J. 2019. "Why teaching classics can stop the spread of the alt-right". *The Sydney Morning Herald*, 24 September. Accessed 28 July 2022. https://www.smh.com.au/education/why-teaching-classics-can-stop-the-spread-of-the-alt-right-20190923-p52u1e.html.

Goff, B. 2005. *Classics and Colonialism*. London: Bloomsbury.

Hall, E. 2019. "Classics for the people". *Aeon*. Accessed 21 April 2021. https://www.theguardian.com/books/2015/jun/20/classics-for-the-people-ancient-greeks.

Hunt, S. 2018. "Getting Classics into Schools? Classics and the Social Justice Agenda of the Coalition Government 2010-2015". In *Forward with Classics: Classical languages in schools and communities*, edited by A. Holmes-Henderson, S. Hunt and M. Musie, 9–26. London: Bloomsbury.

Hunt, S. and A. Holmes-Henderson. 2021. "A level Classics poverty: Classical subjects in schools in England: access, attainment and progression". *Bulletin of the Council of University Classics Departments* 50: 1–26.

Koutsoris, G., L. Stentiford and G. Norwich. 2022. "A critical exploration of inclusion policies of elite UK universities". *British Educational Research Journal* 48: 878–895.

Oliver, M. 2013. "The social model of disability: thirty years on". *Disability & Society* 28 (7): 1024–1026.

Zuckerburg, D. 2018. *Not all dead white men*. Cambridge: Harvard University Press.

1 Ancient languages for 6- to 11-year-olds

Exploring three pedagogical approaches via a longitudinal study

Arlene Holmes-Henderson

Introduction

The Classics in Communities project is a partnership of the University of Oxford, the University of Cambridge and The Iris Project.[1] It was set up by Dr Mai Musié and Dr Evelien Bracke in response to the primary education curriculum reforms which were implemented in England from September 2014. In the Key Stage 2 (KS2) Languages curriculum policy, for the first time, Ancient Greek and Latin were included as appropriate for study by pupils aged 6–11 in place of a modern foreign language. At the same time, English spelling, punctuation and grammar were given a new level of importance within the literacy curriculum. There was a rhetorical shift towards the 'knowledge-based' curriculum and 'rigour' in curriculum design. In some ways, this policy direction benefited ancient languages. But there were very few teachers in primary schools who had, themselves, been taught Latin (and even fewer who had been taught Ancient Greek) at school, so the project had twin aims: to equip teachers in primary schools with the skills and knowledge necessary to teach these languages, and to conduct parallel research to determine the impact of ancient language learning on children's English literacy development (Holmes-Henderson 2016). I joined the project in 2014 as a part-time, fixed-term postdoctoral researcher, as did an administrative assistant. I was principal investigator from 2016 to 2022.

The project provided schools and teachers with information and guidance about teaching approaches and methods, as well as offering classroom resources (Holmes-Henderson 2017). Step-by-step guides on how to introduce Latin and/or Ancient Greek to a primary school, pedagogical videos and learning progression grids were produced and shared freely on the Classics in Communities website to help teachers

DOI: 10.4324/9781003181958-2

monitor how students' skills improved over the course of learning Latin[2] in line with the national languages curriculum expectations for their age. The project brought together primary-, secondary- and higher education-level teachers, helping to create and develop self-sustaining networks of educators committed to sharing their knowledge and expertise. Academics in universities supported experienced and non-experienced teachers of classical languages via training days and workshops 'to establish open channels of communication for knowledge exchange across educational phases' (Holmes-Henderson et al. 2018, 2). Enthusiastic 'non-specialist' teachers committed to significant professional development in order to learn enough Latin and Ancient Greek to be able to teach the languages to young people as part of the curriculum. The initial training day was followed up with classroom observation, further training and regular support. Based at the University of Oxford, the project hosted four international conferences (Holmes-Henderson and Mitropoulos 2016; Holmes-Henderson et al. 2018) and produced a well-reviewed book, *Forward with Classics: Classical languages in Schools and Communities* (Bloomsbury) in 2018. The team won Oxford University Vice-Chancellor's awards in 2019 and 2020.

Research design

In the first longitudinal study of the twenty-first century to examine the impact of learning ancient languages on young children's English literacy, I collated quantitative English literacy (reading and writing) attainment data in partnership with The Iris Project and The Latin Programme. Baseline and progress scores were collected on an annual basis, but to get a fuller understanding of the impact of learning Latin (and Ancient Greek in a small number of schools) beyond literacy attainment alone, qualitative research methods (questionnaires, interviews and focus groups) were used in school visits to hear the situated perspectives of key stakeholders, including pupils, teachers, school leaders and parents.

There are multiple approaches for teaching Latin and Ancient Greek in primary schools (Holmes-Henderson and Kelly 2022). This study compares three. Firstly, The Latin Programme is a charitable organisation which offers lessons from qualified subject specialists (the teachers have Classics degrees) who are trained teachers. Schools pay for lessons from experienced teachers who visit several schools. Secondly, The Iris Project is a charitable organisation which offers lessons from subject specialists (the teachers are university Classics student volunteers) but are not qualified teachers. Lessons are free to schools, but universities subsidise the programme to allow students to visit schools in order to teach weekly lessons during university term time. Thirdly, Classics in Communities, whose teachers are not subject specialists (they learn Latin and/or Ancient Greek as part of their continuing professional development) but are qualified teachers. Training is free to the teachers, and they are the contracted classroom teachers who have an existing relationship with pupils. Ancient languages in this third approach are therefore taught as part of the curriculum by the classroom teacher. Pupils' results have not been compared between these approaches using standard benchmarks as it would be impossible to control for the number of variables. Instead, each approach is evaluated independently, using the available quantitative and/or qualitative data.

Approach one: subject specialists and trained teachers – The Latin Programme

The Latin Programme's specialist peripatetic teachers deliver Latin lessons to London state school pupils in mixed-ability, whole-class groups to help them 'attain higher literacy levels and thereby improve their life chances' since 'learning Latin dramatically broadens students' vocabulary while deepening their understanding of English grammar' (Wing-Davey 2018, 117).

In 2011, The Latin Programme received a three-year grant from SHINE (Support and Help in Education, a national charity) to expand significantly and to undertake a research study by collecting literacy data from schools. Findings were positive: after three years of The Latin Programme, 98 per cent of pupils were reaching the expected level for reading and 91 per cent for writing. By 2016–2017, The Latin Programme was delivering Latin to 1470 children across 49 classes and 9 London boroughs from Camden to Hackney, Brent to Southwark. In total, five teachers from The Latin Programme delivered 9,310 hours of Latin instruction over the course of the school year. In questionnaires distributed to pupils during the programme, many specifically commented on their enjoyment of lessons and on the usefulness of Latin for their learning in other subjects.

Even after the end of the period funded by SHINE, The Latin Programme continued to reach 1036 state school pupils across 37 classes spanning the breadth of Greater London in 2018–2019. Charity staff provided a number of free or subsidised extra-curricular activities and events, such as a writing competition, a Summer School and various storytelling events. They continued to 'dismantle the fallacy that Latin and Classics are subjects only suitable for higher-level ability groups and the privileged elite ... [and] to deconstruct the imposing and daunting grandeur of Classics' (Wing-Davey 2018, 123). They use the 'Via Facilis' curriculum.

The Latin Programme takes a comparative approach by looking at Latin through the lens of English grammar rather than the reading-based style of many Latin textbooks. The aim is that students gain 'a mechanism for investigating and understanding grammatical structures, for getting used to analysing and questioning how language works, how and why linguistic patterns matter, and to get students used to the idea that there are patterns in their own language, even if they are not directly relatable to Latin grammar' (Wing-Davey 2018, 118). The Latin Programme offers schools a two-for-one: both literacy and foreign-language provision are covered (Latin 'counts' on the KS2 Languages curriculum, so there is no need for schools to teach another language). There is bonus content too: 'using our curriculum as a foundation, each teacher designs bespoke lessons that bring in music, movement, drama and even cookery to allow our pupils to flex their creative muscles and build the confidence, creativity and resilience that are of vital importance in adult life' (The Latin Programme 2020, 3). The Programme therefore is focussed not only on improving literacy results but also on cultivating individuality, diversity and creativity.

Methodology

During the SHINE-funded period (2011–2014), The Latin Programme requested data from all schools.

Once all anonymised pupil data were collated, the next stage involved developing a consistent approach to measuring progress from an initial baseline, using a single literacy score. Scores took the form of alphanumeric levels and sub-levels to measure progress as was commonplace under the curricular framework at the time. However, a number of schools had provided two separate scores for reading and writing; these needed to be averaged and then converted into a single, alphanumeric literacy score. The initial conversion matrix used in this process calculated the average of the two reading and writing scores. In the instances where an average could not be taken easily, for example a reading score of 2b and a writing score of 2c, a formula was added to select a random value within the parameters, for example a 50 per cent chance of a 2b score and a 50 per cent chance of a 2c score.

In order to calculate the alphanumeric values to measure progress from baseline scores, a numeric value was added to the a, b and c

12 *Arlene Holmes-Henderson*

sub-levels, consistent with the literacy conversion score, ascending from the lowest score of 1 assigned to level 1c up to the maximum score of 18 for level 6a. This then provided a simple methodology to calculate any progress made across sub-levels. For example, if a pupil provided a baseline score of 2b and recorded a progress score of 4c, this would represent five sub-levels of progress. This was successfully validated by subtracting the 2b score of 5 from the 4c score of 10; this would also provide a measure of five sub-levels of progress.

A process was then undertaken to identify unique pupils by concatenating anonymised pupil name and school. This provided a unique text string that was able to identify individual anonymised pupils, which was then validated by correlating school year with academic year.

Sub-levels of literacy progress

Using all data collected, of the pupils who participated in The Latin Programme, 86.4 per cent achieved progress, with 68.8 per cent achieving two or more sub-levels of progress (Figure 1.1). Two sub-levels of progress per academic year is considered good (Department for Education 2011). Over a fifth (22.2 per cent) achieved four or more sub-levels of progress. Here it is worth noting two things: (1) some pupils made no progress and others regressed. These results reflect the students who started the programme but left the school, were persistent absentees or who could not access the course content

Sub-Levels of Literacy Progress

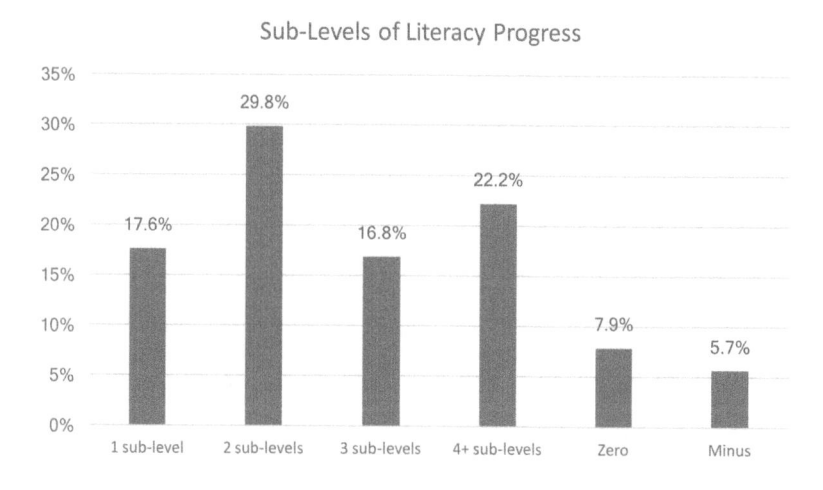

Category	Percentage
1 sub-level	17.6%
2 sub-levels	29.8%
3 sub-levels	16.8%
4+ sub-levels	22.2%
Zero	7.9%
Minus	5.7%

Figure 1.1 Progress by all pupils.

for a variety of other reasons, and (2) the schools which participated in the SHINE-funded project were chosen because they included a high number of disadvantaged pupils. The majority of pupils in these schools had not previously made any progress and were far short of achieving their age-related expectations. To see several pupils making significant gains in literacy was 'a dream come true' according to one Year Five teacher.

Progress of pupils by duration of programme

What was the optimal time period to participate in The Latin Programme teaching for improved literacy scores? There were significant gains for most pupils after one year and more significant gains after two years.

In total, 60.8 per cent of pupils participating in The Latin Programme for one year made two or more sub-levels of progress (Figure 1.2). This compares to 95.3 per cent of pupils who attended for two years and 81.3 per cent who attended for three years. Interestingly, 71.9 per cent of pupils who attended The Latin Programme for three years achieved four or more sub-levels of progress. It is important to note, however, that there are much larger sample sizes for pupils who attended for one (485) or two years (150) than those who attended for three (32) years.

Progress of Pupils by Duration (years) of Programme

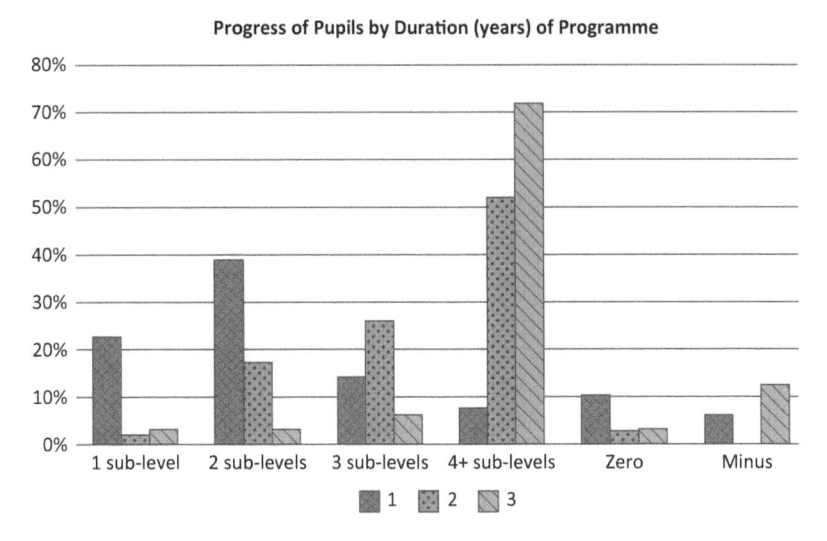

Figure 1.2 Progress of pupils by duration (years) of attending The Latin Programme.

When segmenting the data, there are three interesting trends which deserve special mention. The Latin Programme's cohort included a significantly higher than average number of pupils eligible for Free School Meals (FSM), 30.6 per cent. The national average for primary pupils was 15.6 per cent (Department for Education 2015a). It is well attested that the attainment gap between children eligible and not eligible for FSM is apparent at the age of seven: 62 per cent and 80 per cent, respectively, reached the 'expected level' in the national reading and writing tests. Essentially, the literacy gap is 18 per cent (Demie and McLean 2019, 1).

Sub-levels of progress by pupils eligible for FSM

It is illuminating, then, that when learning English literacy through Latin, there was no such attainment gap for pupils eligible for FSM in The Latin Programme's sample (Figure 1.3). Of the 700 pupils who participated in this part of the study, 68.8 per cent of both FSM-eligible and pupils not eligible for FSM achieved two or more sub-levels of progress. However, a higher proportion of pupils eligible for FSM made two sub-levels of progress than non-FSM pupils, whereas a slightly higher proportion of non-FSM pupils made three sub-levels of progress compared to FSM-eligible pupils. When asked about

Sub-Levels of Progress by FSM-eligible Pupils

	FSM-eligible Pupils	Non-FSM-eligible Pupils
4+ sub-levels	22.0%	22.3%
3 sub-levels	14.1%	18.0%
2 sub-levels	32.7%	28.5%
1 sub-level	14.6%	18.9%

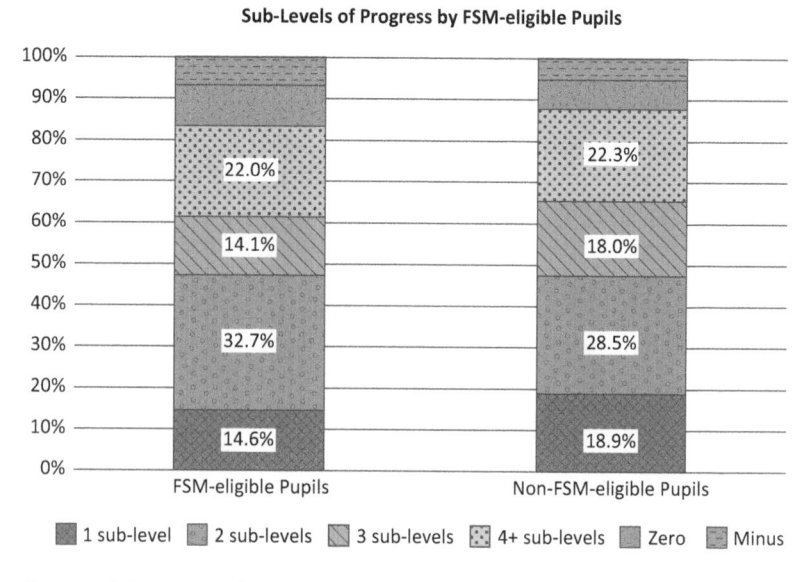

■ 1 sub-level ■ 2 sub-levels ■ 3 sub-levels ■ 4+ sub-levels ■ Zero ■ Minus

Figure 1.3 Progress of FSM-eligible and non-FSM-eligible pupils.

the disappearance of the attainment gap in literacy for FSM-eligible pupils, teachers commented that learners were able to apply knowledge gained in Latin to support their reading and writing across the curriculum. Etymology and morphology were commonly referenced by teachers as foundations which paved the way for improved reading comprehension and, in turn, better quality English writing (also mentioned in Quigley 2018, 62). In qualitative research engagements, pupils said.

> 'It's really useful for literacy, extending vocabulary and grammar and the derivation of words' and 'It's helped me so much with confidence and with other subjects'.

Special Educational Needs (SEN)[3]

'A pupil has SEN where their learning difficulty or disability calls for special educational provision, namely provision different from or additional to that normally available to pupils of the same age' (Department for Education 2015b, 94–95). In this sample, the four broad areas of learner needs were represented (Department for Education 2015b): communication and interaction; cognition and learning; social, emotional and mental health difficulties; and sensory and/or physical needs. In total, 21.6 per cent (145) of pupils in the sample had been identified by their schools as having SEN, in comparison to 78.4 per cent (526) with no SEN. Again, this is higher than the national average for the primary sector in England for the time under analysis which was 17.9 per cent. A recent Department for Education literature review of SEN and disability education estimated the attainment gap at 52 per cent (Department for Education 2020a). In total, 22 per cent of pupils with SEN achieved the expected level in reading, writing and mathematics in 2018/2019 compared to 74 per cent of those with no SEN. This attainment gap of 52 per cent was not visible in The Latin Programme's literacy data.

Sub-levels of progress by pupils with SEN

In total, 62.1 per cent of pupils with SEN made two or more sub-levels of progress, compared with 70.7 per cent of pupils with no SEN (Figure 1.4). It appears that learners with SEN made similar progress to peers with no SEN when learning literacy through Latin. In this study, the attainment gap looks more like eight per cent. Pupil feedback is illuminating here:

Sub-Levels of Progress by Pupils with SEN

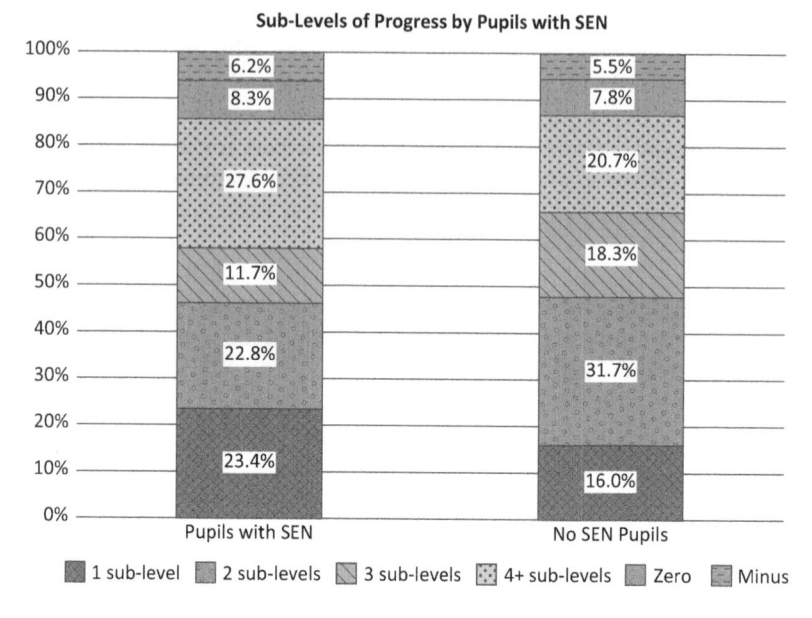

Pupils with SEN:
- 1 sub-level: 23.4%
- 2 sub-levels: 22.8%
- 3 sub-levels: 11.7%
- 4+ sub-levels: 27.6%
- Zero: 8.3%
- Minus: 6.2%

No SEN Pupils:
- 1 sub-level: 16.0%
- 2 sub-levels: 31.7%
- 3 sub-levels: 18.3%
- 4+ sub-levels: 20.7%
- Zero: 7.8%
- Minus: 5.5%

Figure 1.4 Progress of pupils with SEN and No SEN pupils.

'It has helped me with my spelling and understanding longer more complicated words'; 'I usually find learning new languages quite hard but with Latin I understood everything' and 'I really like how you don't have to worry about saying it a particular way. It takes the pressure off and I feel more confident to speak up'.

English as an Additional Language (EAL)

In the Latin Programme's London-based project, just over half (50.7 per cent) of pupils spoke English as an Additional Language. This was significantly above the national average of 28 per cent, during the period under study (Department for Education 2020b). At the end of Reception, only 44 per cent of pupils recorded as having EAL achieve a good level of development, compared to 54 per cent of pupils recorded as First Language English (L1 English) (Strand et al. 2015). The attainment gap for six- to nine-year-olds is often estimated at ten per cent.

Sub-levels of progress by pupils with EAL

In total, 67.1 per cent of pupils with EAL achieved two or more sub-levels of progress compared to 70.7 per cent of pupils with L1 English (Figure 1.5). When learning literacy through Latin with The

Sub-Levels of Progress by Pupils with EAL

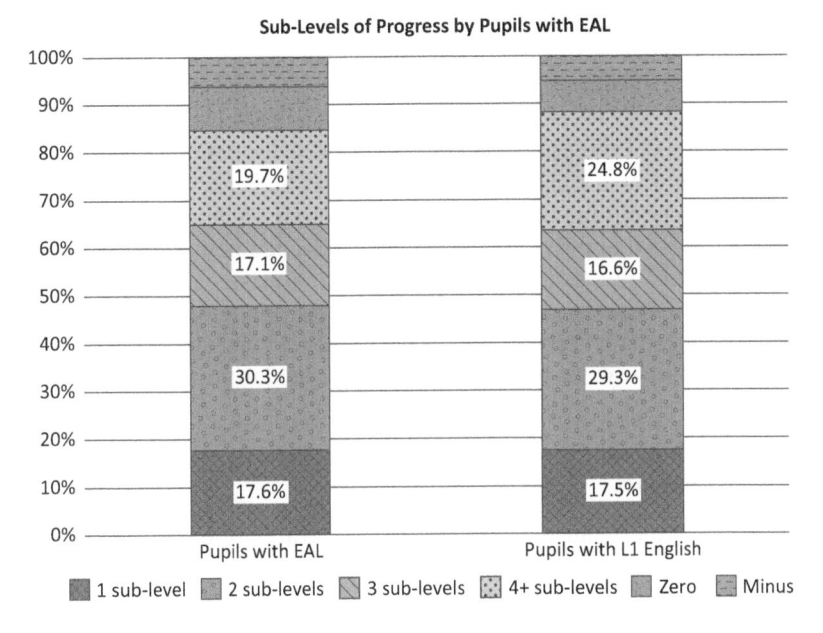

Category	Pupils with EAL	Pupils with L1 English
4+ sub-levels	19.7%	24.8%
3 sub-levels	17.1%	16.6%
2 sub-levels	30.3%	29.3%
1 sub-level	17.6%	17.5%

Legend: 1 sub-level, 2 sub-levels, 3 sub-levels, 4+ sub-levels, Zero, Minus

Figure 1.5 Progress of pupils with EAL and pupils with L1 English.

Latin Programme, the gap was much smaller (three per cent). Pupils with EAL regularly made comments such as:

> I love Latin because there are so many Latin words that are the same in Portuguese;
>
> 'It has helped me with my English and I like the help it gives me'
>
> 'I love how the words follow patterns. When the teacher explains how the Latin grammar works, it helps me understand English better'.

Discussing the range of languages spoken by learners in the class provides opportunities for linguistic and cultural enrichment. Sleeter (1991) suggests that 'When students can identify with the curriculum being taught, their voices become empowered and they establish a firm ground for their self-identity'.

Feedback from one headteacher underlines the literacy support that Latin offers teachers and pupils with EAL:

> 'We need more support with language links – with romance languages and crucially, with the English language. Not all teachers know a diversity of root words or realise the importance of

understanding the meanings behind a wider range of suffix and prefix work. This kind of learning with a pattern supports all children, but particularly EAL children'.

The national inspection agency, Ofsted (2020), commented on the contribution of Latin to the curriculum at St Peter's Eaton Square primary school (one of The Latin Programme's schools in London), 'Pupils like using previous knowledge to decode new words in Latin and English. For example, pupils in Year 6 easily worked out the meaning of words such as "pugnacious" and "necromancy" in a text and could explain their origin …. They also told me how much it helps them with their work in other subjects, particularly English'.

Approach two: subject specialists and volunteers –
The Iris Project

The Iris Project, an educational charity, trains undergraduate students to introduce the languages and cultures of the ancient world to primary school students. They deliver weekly 'literacy through Latin' lessons on the curriculum in state-maintained primary schools. The Project particularly targets schools in deprived regions of the UK, where literacy levels can be low, and many children are eligible for FSM. Since 2006, The Project has worked with thousands of pupils and hundreds of schools to improve literacy, confidence and enjoyment of languages. The Literacy through Latin project operates in Edinburgh, Fife, Glasgow, London, Manchester, Oxford, Reading and Swansea with a dedicated headquarters at the Community Classics Centre and Rumble Museum based at Cheney School in East Oxford.

> 'Learning Latin is a brilliant way to support children's literacy. It helps children make connections between Latin and English grammar and vocabulary and gives them the key to unlock English'.
> (Lorna Robinson, Founder of The Iris Project)

The work of The Iris Project has been praised by Ofsted (2011) too. An inspection report for St Saviour's Church of England Primary School in Brixton noted that 'the school has a range of effective partnerships with external agencies, including The Iris Project with King's College London which, by teaching Year 5 pupils Latin, has made a strong contribution to those pupils' improved writing'.

The project hosts a number of free resources on its website and has published two textbooks for use in primary schools: *Telling Tales in*

Greek (Robinson 2017) takes the reader on a journey through tales from Homer's *Iliad* and the *Odyssey*. Along the way, readers pick up the Greek alphabet, words and grammar and are encouraged to explore the connections between Greek and English. This illustrated Greek course reads like a story book and, as such, appeals to a wide range of learners. Every chapter leads readers through the tales, exploring new aspects of grammar, and ends with suggestions for activities, as well as ways in which the story can be explored from literary and creative perspectives. Emphasis is placed upon thinking about the resonance of mythical stories and identifying why these stories developed.

Telling Tales in Latin (Robinson 2013) takes the reader on an adventure through tales from Ovid's *Metamorphoses*. This story book appeals to a wide range of learners and explores the connections between Latin and English, as well as other languages. Like its Greek twin, every chapter leads readers through the tales, exploring new aspects of grammar, and ends with suggestions for activities, as well as ways in which the story can be explored from literary and creative perspectives. The book also encourages readers to think about the many ways in which the stories connect to modern ideas, including themes such as scientific advances, climate change and caring for the planet. Alongside these cross-curricular connections, there is a continual focus on literacy and language.

The charity receives no core funding, so their work relies on volunteer effort and donations. The Classics Postgraduate Certificate in Education (PGCE) course at King's College London works with The Iris Project to provide formal teacher-training for student volunteers. Funding has been provided by a range of individuals and organisations, including the Cambridge University School Classics Project, Classics Conclave, Royal Holloway Classics Society, the Hellenic Society, University College London, The Esmée Fairbairn Foundation, Friends of Classics, Oxford University Classics Faculty, The Winton Charitable Foundation, Trinity College Cambridge, King's College London, Mercers' Charitable Foundation, The Gavron Trust and The Hamilton Trust.

Impact on pupils' literacy

Working in partnership with the Iris Project, we analysed data collected from three primary schools over three years 2010–2013, all in areas of high socio-economic disadvantage. In School One, 46 children learned Latin on timetable at KS2 for two years. In total, 67 per cent of these children attending School One achieved their predicted or a better grade in reading. In total, 74 per cent of children achieved their predicted grade (or better) in writing, with almost 50 per cent of the children achieving a grade beyond their prediction.

In School Two, 55 children learned Latin on timetable at KS2 over two academic years. In total, 80 per cent of children attending School Two achieved their predicted grade (or better) in reading. In total, 71 per cent of children achieved their predicted grade (or better) in writing.

In School Three, 53 children learned Latin on timetable at KS2 over two academic years. In total, 96 per cent of children attending School Three achieved their predicted grade (or better) in reading. In total, 94 per cent of children achieved their predicted grade (or better) in writing.

It is, of course, extremely difficult to make a direct causal link between the study of Latin and improved English reading and writing grades. These pupils were learning literacy as a core component of the curriculum and were reading English in topics across the curriculum. They summarised the impact in a number of ways:

> 'I think Latin lessons are fun and it helps me with other languages';
>
> 'At first I thought it was going to be rubbish because it's a dead language, but it turned out to be quite fun';
>
> 'Latin is helpful for working out the meaning of unfamiliar words. You can sometimes spot the root, or you know the meaning of a prefix and that's so helpful for SATs'.

There were a number of positive comments about the student volunteers and their teaching:

> 'the teacher was good';
>
> 'very fun teacher';
>
> 'I have learned a lot: thank you for teaching me great lessons.'

There was also some feedback which exposed their inexperience:

> 'I would enjoy it if there was more control over the class';
>
> 'It was really good to learn about but some people spoilt it';
>
> 'Latin lessons were fun but the teacher sometimes made mistakes; no one is perfect'.

The volunteers themselves provided feedback on the experience:

> 'I enjoyed my involvement with The Iris Project and as a medical student I loved the opportunity it afforded me to exercise my creative streak. Unfortunately, next year I will be a final year medical student and for our final year we are given placements outside London (anywhere from Dorset to the Outer Hebrides!) so I don't think it would be feasible to continue in a London school next year'.
> (Fifth Year Medical student, London)

> 'I am going to do a PGCE next year based on my positive experience of teaching with The Iris Project this year. I will recommend it to my peers on the undergraduate Classics course'.
> (Final year undergraduate classicist, London)

Approach three: trained teachers and non-specialists –
Classics in Communities

Given that the 2014 KS2 Languages curriculum reform expressly named Latin and Ancient Greek as languages suitable for study in the primary phase, the Classics in Communities project sought to equip primary teachers, through training events, with the subject knowledge and confidence they needed to teach Latin and Ancient Greek in their schools. In 2014–2015, one-day teacher training workshops were held at King's College London, the University of Oxford, the University of Cambridge, Lordswood School Birmingham, the University of Glasgow and Queen's University Belfast. These initial training days brought together 45 primary teachers interested in (but previously unfamiliar with) teaching Latin and Ancient Greek with experienced teachers and academics.

This cross-sectoral structure was selected to ensure a degree of self-sustainability in the regions – it was crucial for primary teachers to meet experienced teachers and academics so that they felt supported in their new classical adventure. Equally, secondary teachers and academics in universities enjoyed the opportunity for dialogue and were keen to establish open channels of communication for knowledge exchange across educational phases. The events were publicised to the local educational authorities by the local University, by the University of Oxford central outreach team and by the Classics in Communities project (by email and through social media). The cost of the workshops was £40, but full bursaries were available for teachers, thanks to the generosity of the Society for the Promotion of Roman Studies

22 *Arlene Holmes-Henderson*

and the Society for the Promotion of Hellenic Studies. Glasgow was the most popular venue, with 22 participants. Belfast had the fewest attendees, just five. The training day was broadly divided into two: Latin in the morning and Ancient Greek in the afternoon.

After a welcome from the local host and an introduction from the Classics in Communities team, the likely benefits of teaching Latin in the primary classroom were discussed (based on research studies to date), as were some of the challenges of setting up a new language in a school. Participants had the opportunity to try out some Latin learning of their own, and they asked a number of questions about which pedagogical approaches were suitable for teaching a classical language. The final session before lunch was a 30-minute talk from an experienced local primary teacher who outlined their top tips for introducing Latin. The cascade of this information from a fellow teacher who had actually been through the process was particularly valuable for participants and allowed them to have many practical questions answered.

The afternoon was spent introducing teachers to the Ancient Greek alphabet and helping them to transliterate. Exercises exploring vocabulary, derivations and present tense verbs gave them a flavour of the content of Ancient Greek at KS2 level. Various resources were shared, and their suitability for use with children at KS2 level was discussed.

Feedback from teachers

Questionnaires were distributed to all participants in the training workshops. The first was completed at the end of the training day, and another was sent electronically six months later. The feedback from the teachers highlighted a number of interesting findings which have been important for subsequent phases of the project.

The collated results show that, at the end of the one-day training event, 70 per cent of survey respondees said it was 'very likely' that they would start teaching Latin in their primary schools (Figure 1.6). In total, 13 per cent said it was 'likely' and 17 per cent replied 'maybe'. Not a single participant replied 'probably not' or 'definitely not'.

The picture for Ancient Greek was much less encouraging (Figure 1.7). Only 22 per cent of primary teachers thought it 'very likely' that they would introduce Ancient Greek. In total, nine per cent thought it 'likely', 47 per cent (the majority) replied 'maybe', 16 per cent thought 'probably not' and six per cent had decided that it was 'definitely not' for them. Common reasons given for these less enthusiastic responses included Ancient Greek being harder for the teachers themselves to learn, it being beyond the intellectual reach of some children, and the lack of suitably demanding but engaging textbooks. One

Ancient languages for 6- to 11-year-olds 23

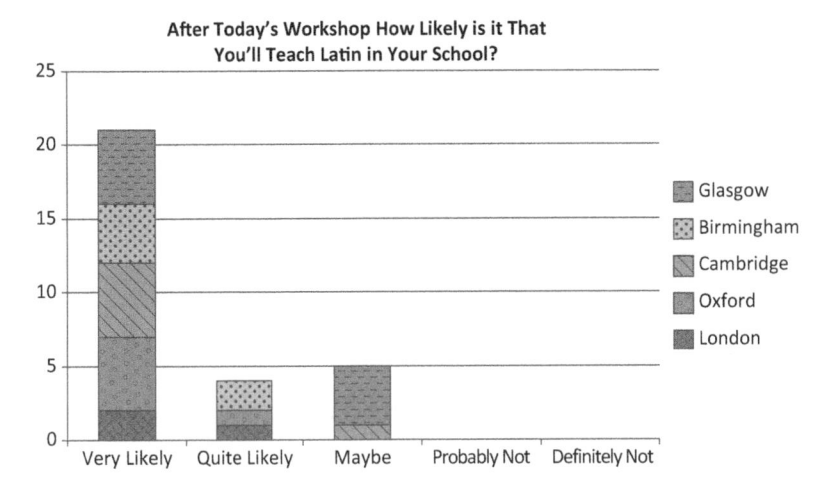

Figure 1.6 End of workshop teacher responses regarding introducing Latin.

teacher commented, 'If I'm finding this hard, there's no way my Year 5s would cope'.

The follow-up questionnaire asked participants to evaluate the impact of the Classics in Communities training day on the language offering at their schools. More than 90 per cent of respondents answered that Latin was now being taught in their school. There were a number of interesting responses in the questionnaires, such as:

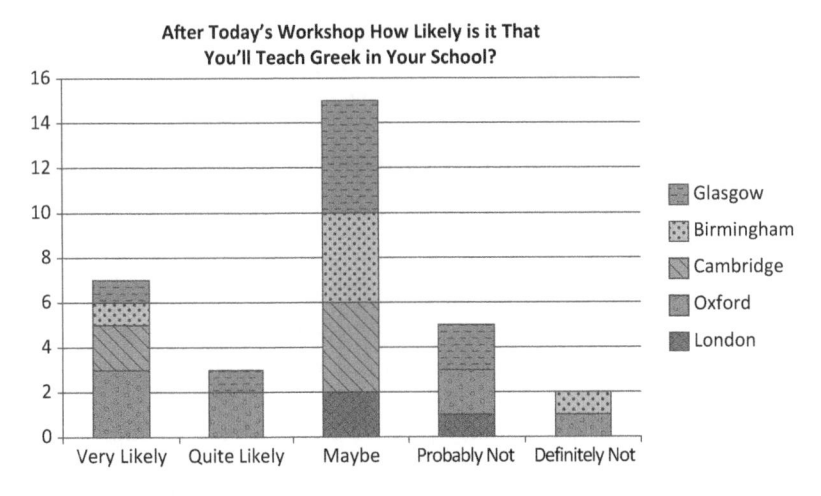

Figure 1.7 End of workshop teacher responses regarding introducing Ancient Greek.

'I have learnt alongside the children – a good confidence builder. The children know I am not an expert so we are all on a level playing field and this gives them a boost in confidence';

'I feel as if I have achieved a new skill and it is something which I really enjoy and love learning about';

'It has introduced me to a language which I had never considered it possible to get even a simple grasp of' and

'I was surprised that it could appeal so strongly to children'.

Headteachers said:

'it has given the children a different challenge and something new' and

'Latin has contributed significantly to enriching our curriculum' and

'Learning Latin with Minimus (Bell 1999) the mouse brings a breath of fresh air to our children'.

Feedback from parents

In a focus group with parents held in an area of rural socio-economic disadvantage, many indicated that they were surprised when they heard that their children's school was teaching Latin. One said,

'I thought my kid was having a laugh when he told me. Latin? Why would the school be teaching that? All them Romans are dead'. Another added, 'I must admit I thought it was an odd choice. I had hoped that the school would teach [child's name] Spanish, as it's the most widely spoken language in the world, isn't it?'.

However, as the discussion developed, parents reflected:

'I wasn't taught Latin at school and I'm pleased that they have the chance. They seem to love it';

'I wasn't at all sure at the start but he's a right little Latin fan now';

'To be honest, I don't think [child's name] really likes the Latin at all but they love all the myths, stories and gladiators'.

The feedback was particularly positive from parents of pupils with EAL and SEN. Both groups identified that Latin 'levelled the playing field' more than modern languages and provided support for English literacy across the curriculum.

Ancient Greek at Key Stage 2

In the follow-up questionnaire, one teacher, based in the East of England, reported that they were teaching Ancient Greek at KS2 after attending a Classics in Communities training workshop in November 2015. This teacher had studied Ancient Greek at university and so had secure subject knowledge:

> 'To facilitate the teaching of Classical Greek, the students in Key Stage 2 learnt in streamed Literacy groups that are different to their usual Form classes. All of Year 6 accessed Greek in the academic year 2015-16 and all of Year 5 did in 2016-17. The students who were not taught Classical Greek at first accessed it when they reached a higher year group and greater Literacy attainment; all of the students in Key Stage 2 learn Classical Greek during their time at the school. This means that close to 200 children, as of July 2019, have already accessed a Classical language thanks to Classics in Communities.
>
> Our twice annual data, compiled through INCAs assessment, shows that learning Classical Greek has improved English Reading Comprehension, Spelling, Word Reading and Word Decoding for the pupils. This is a demonstrable impact for these children who have accessed a Classical language'.[4]

This finding appears to support recently published results from a study in Greece: pupils aged 6 to 9 who learned Ancient Greek for two hours per week had statistically improved visual-perceptual and cognitive skills which enabled better performance at school (Manolidou et al. 2022).

This teacher in the East of England became increasingly enthused about Ancient Greek and sought out opportunities to develop Classics across the curriculum. They set up a project called The Arts Award, in partnership with a local museum, using the British Museum's amphora vase depicting what is believed to be a Panathenaic horserace. The Arts Award combined pupils' skills in Reading comprehension, Literacy performance and presentation, Computing animation, Historical analysis, Art and Design and Technology (craft and composition), Art History investigation and Greek language. At the end of the project, each pupil received an Entry Level Qualification in Art History. To begin the learning, the pupils 'excavated' like archaeologists and found broken pieces of a pot decorated like the vase. This vase was inspired by 'The Cheat', an animation project produced by The Panoply Vase Project.

The teacher described the impact on their practice:

'I have learned how language and role-playing could bring a distant time and place to life in the classroom to support high levels of attainment for all pupils, regardless of background or previous attainment levels'. The benefits to pupils, in this case, stretched beyond learning the Ancient Greek alphabet to 'improving links within the community, as they have worked with the museum, and presented their completed vase animations in a public and community school assembly'.

Limitations

There are a number of limitations which must be considered when evaluating the data generated by this investigation. I have evaluated only three pedagogical approaches for teaching Latin and Ancient Greek in primary classrooms: many more exist (Holmes-Henderson et al. 2018, Holmes-Henderson and Kelly 2022). The Latin Programme's request for data was answered by a small pool of the schools with which it worked during the SHINE-funded period. There are, of course, many other primary schools in urban and rural settings across the UK which teach classical languages (British Council 2022). The sample size was moderate (approximately 2000 pupils), included schools in urban, coastal and rural locations, but did not include a control group.

The responses in questionnaires distributed at the end of the Classics in Communities training days might indicate 'acquiescence bias' (Chung 2022), where teachers have indicated, out of politeness, that they're likely to teach Latin in their classrooms. They may have felt that this was the right thing to do after an enjoyable training day. The response rate to the follow-up questionnaire was much lower than to the original question (about a third), and those who replied were likely to be the very people who wanted to share good news.

The student questionnaires were delivered by teachers and/or student volunteers at the schools. The activities conducted before, or promised after questionnaire completion, were likely to influence results, as would peer influence. Not all classes in each school were included: some students were absent, some year groups were out of school (on study leave, exchange visits, etc.) and therefore unavailable. The data, even within these schools, is limited.

Although I was able to conduct headteacher, teacher and parent interviews in a separate, quiet room, there were disturbances (bells and noise indicating a change of lessons or end of the school day) and the interviewees' own – often very limited – time available for my questioning. In many cases, the teachers would have liked the time to speak about their ancient languages provision at much greater length but had to attend to their duties within the school. However, this type of data is helpful towards understanding some of the lived experiences of individuals involved in teaching and learning Latin and Ancient Greek in primary schools.

Suggestions for future research

This study has produced promising results which indicate that there is a positive correlation between the study of Latin and improved English literacy attainment, especially for students who fall into three categories of educational disadvantage: SEN, FSM and EAL. Feedback on the introduction of Latin to the curriculum from teachers, student volunteers, headteachers and parents has been largely positive. A more ambitious study is needed to test these findings at scale and to compare pedagogical approaches using a unified assessment framework. It will be interesting to filter results by morphology, syntax, comprehension and orthography to better understand the details of Latin's influence on English literacy attainment.

Notes

1 Funding for the project was provided by the University of Oxford, the University of Cambridge, the Classical Association, the Institute of Classical Studies and the A.G. Leventis Foundation.
2 Latin and Ancient Greek enjoy parity of esteem in the KS2 Languages curriculum, but feedback from teachers, early in the Classics in Communities project, made clear that Latin was a more popular choice than Ancient Greek.
3 For further information on terminology, see Cullen et al. (2020). There is a large degree of overlap between disability, as defined by the Equality Act 2010, and special educational needs, as defined in the Children and Families Act 2014 (Department for Education 2015b, 16). SEN has been chosen here because this is the terminology used in the policies of the schools participating in the study.
4 A diagnostic, adaptive assessment for children aged 5–11 years – see https://www.cem.org/incas.

Reference List

Bell, B. 1999. *Minimus: Starting out in Latin*. Cambridge: Cambridge University Press.

British Council. 2022. "Languages Trends 2022: Language Teaching in primary and secondary schools in England". Accessed 27 July 2022. https://www.britishcouncil.org/sites/default/files/language_trends_report_2022.pdf.

Chung, L. 2022. "The 7 types of sampling and response bias to avoid in customer surveys". Accessed 28 February 2022. https://delighted.com/blog/avoid-7-types-sampling-response-survey-bias.

Cullen, M. A., G. Lindsay, R. Hastings, L. Denne, C. Stanford, L. Beqiraq, F. Elahi, E. Gemegah, N. Hayden, I. Kander, F. Lykomitrou and J. Zander. 2020. *Special Educational Needs in Mainstream Schools: Evidence Review*. London: Educational Endowment Foundation. Accessed 28 February 2022. https://educationendowmentfoundation.org.uk/public/files/Publications/Send/EEF_SEND_Evidence_Review.pdf.

Demie, F. and C. McLean. 2019. "Tackling Educational Disadvantage. What Works in Schools". Accessed 28 February 2022. https://www.lambeth.gov.uk/sites/default/files/2021-05/tackling_educational_disadvantage_-_what_works_in_schools.pdf.

Department for Education. 2011. "How do pupils progress during Key Stages 2 and 3?". DFE-RR096. Accessed 28 February 2022. https://assets.publishing.service.gov.uk/government/uploads/system/uploads/attachment_data/file/182413/DFE-RR096.pdf.

Department for Education. 2015a. "Statistical First Release: Schools, Pupils and Their Characteristics: January 2015". Accessed 28 February 2022. https://assets.publishing.service.gov.uk/government/uploads/system/uploads/attachment_data/file/433680/SFR16_2015_Main_Text.pdf.

Department for Education. 2015b. "Special educational needs and disabilities Code of Practice, 0-25 Years". DFE-00205-2013. Accessed 28 February 2022. https://www.gov.uk/government/publications/send-code-of-practice-0-to-25

Department for Education. 2020a. "Special educational needs and disability: an analysis and summary of data sources". Accessed 28 February 2022. https://explore-education-statistics.service.gov.uk/find-statistics/special-educational-needs-in-england/2019-20.

Department for Education. 2020b. "English proficiency of pupils with English as an additional language". Accessed 28 February 2022. https://assets.publishing.service.gov.uk/government/uploads/system/uploads/attachment_data/file/868209/English_proficiency_of_EAL_pupils.pdf.

Holmes-Henderson, A. 2016. "Teaching Latin and Greek in primary classrooms: the Classics in Communities Project". *Journal of Classics Teaching* 17 (33): 50–53. http://dx.doi.org/10.1017/S2058631016000131.

Holmes-Henderson, A. 2017. "Classics in Communities resources for "non-specialist" teachers of Latin and/or Ancient Greek". *Classical Association Blog*, 21 November. Accessed 1 March 2022. http://theclassicalassociation.blogspot.com/2017/11/classics-in-communities-resources-for.html.

Holmes-Henderson, A., S. Hunt and M. Musié. 2018. *Forward with Classics: Classical Languages in Schools and Communities*. London: Bloomsbury.

Holmes-Henderson, A. and K. Kelly. 2022. *Ancient Languages in Primary Schools in England: A Literature Review.* Department for Education. Accessed 17 November 2022. https://assets.publishing.service.gov.uk/government/uploads/system/uploads/attachment_data/file/1120024/Ancient_languages_in_primary_schools_in_England_-_A_Literature_Review.pdf.

Holmes-Henderson, A. and A. Mitropoulos. 2016. "A celebration of Greek language and culture education in the UK". *Journal of Classics Teaching* 17 (34): 55–57. https://doi.org/10.1017/S2058631016000258.

Manolidou, E., S. Goula and V. Sakka. 2022. "Ancient Greek for Kids: From Theory to Praxis". *Journal of Classics Teaching*, 1–9. http://dx.doi.org/10.1017/S2058631022000253.

Ofsted. 2011. "School Inspection Report of St Saviour's Church of England Primary School". 25 November 2011. Accessed 1 March 2022. https://files.ofsted.gov.uk/v1/file/1986999.

Ofsted. 2020. "Subject inspection of St Peter's Eaton Square Church of England Primary School". 9 January 2020. Accessed 1 March 2022. https://files.ofsted.gov.uk/v1/file/50143360.

Quigley, A. 2018. *Closing the Vocabulary Gap.* London: Routledge.

Robinson, L. 2013. *Telling Tales in Latin: A New Latin Course and Storybook for Children.* London: Souvenir Press Ltd.

Robinson, L. 2017. *Telling Tales in Greek.* London: Souvenir Press Ltd.

Sleeter, C. 1991. *Empowerment through multicultural education: Teacher empowerment and school reform.* Albany: State University of New York Press.

Strand, S., L. Malmberg and J. Hall. 2015. "English as an Additional Language (EAL) and educational achievement in England: An analysis of the National Pupil Database". Accessed 28 February 2022. https://ore.exeter.ac.uk/repository/bitstream/handle/10871/23323/EAL_and_educational_achievement2.pdf?sequence=1&isAllowed=y.

The Latin Programme. 2020. "Via Facilis Impact Report: 2019-20". Accessed 28 February 2022. https://static1.squarespace.com/static/5ca3548694d71a2bab77f9d0/t/600ed5d820c2137a1c3ed2d6/1611584992902/Impact+Report+2020+%282%29.pdf.

Wing-Davey, Z. 2018. "Delivering Latin in primary schools". In *Forward with Classics: Languages in Schools and Communities*, edited by A. Holmes-Henderson, S. Hunt and M. Musié, 111–128. London: Bloomsbury.

2 Including the excluded

Teaching Latin in an area of high socio-economic disadvantage

Peter Wright

Socio-economic, geographic and demographic contexts

Blackpool is a town in the North West of England which is famous for tourism. For over 100 years, the Blackpool Pleasure Beach has welcomed thrill-seekers to enjoy the adrenaline rush of its rollercoasters. The Blackpool Illuminations have been enchanting young and old alike since 1879, and the world-famous Blackpool Tower has hosted international ballroom dancing competitions for decades. However, despite Blackpool's reputation as a tourist hotspot, it, like so many other coastal towns, continues to suffer from under-investment and government cuts. According to a 2019 report, 'neighbourhoods in Blackpool ... account for eight of the ten most deprived neighbourhoods nationally' (Ministry of Housing, Communities and Local Government 2019, 5). Social issues within the town are significant, from the challenges faced by transient workers and their families associated with seasonal employment to high levels of poverty, substance abuse and crime. Postcards of Blackpool depict the 'Golden Mile' seafront with happy families on a day out and children eating ice creams. While this does of course happen, the reality of growing up in Blackpool is much less idyllic for hundreds of children. It is within this challenging context that a re-introduction of Latin in the twenty-first century has been both popular and effective. It is hoped that the success and growth of Latin within the Blackpool educational landscape might provide valuable food-for-thought for educators and leaders who are considering the introduction of classical subjects to their own schools and communities.

Access to Classics in Blackpool

The opportunity for students in Blackpool to access Classics, in all its various forms, historically, has been extremely restricted. Prior to 2010, provision for budding classicists was limited to either post-16 study or

DOI: 10.4324/9781003181958-3

attendance at a small number of independent schools. The impact of the 1988 Education Reform Act on Classics provision in Blackpool schools meant that, very rapidly, the only discussion of Latin lessons in local households came from nostalgic conversations with parents and grandparents. The chance to encounter the history and culture of Greeks and Romans came only via brief sequences of learning in primary schools as part of the Key Stage Two curriculum for pupils between 7 and 11 years of age. Despite this, take-up of A-Level Classical Civilisation and A-Level Ancient History at Blackpool Sixth Form College demonstrated that there was an underlying enthusiasm and appetite to investigate the collapse of the Roman Republic, the great architecture of Athens, the epic literature of Homer and other classical topics. The introduction and implementation of the 'Curriculum 2000' post-16 A-Level reform, certainly within the Blackpool context, had a transformative effect in opening up the classical world to local pupils. No longer restricted in A-Level choice, and able to take advantage of an accessible modular structure which encouraged a more holistic and thematic study of the ancient world, numbers of Advanced Subsidiary (AS) and Advanced Level (A2) students at Blackpool Sixth Form College soon exceeded over 200 in each year.[1] Furthermore, for the vast majority of these students, this study represented one of their first detailed encounters with the Greeks, Persians and Romans in formal education.

Resulting from the success of the A-Level programme, in 2016, Blackpool Sixth Form College was contacted by the educational charity Classics for All about an ambitious plan to create regional hubs in order to facilitate the reintroduction of the various forms of Classics (including the study of Ancient History, Classical Civilisation, Ancient Greek and Latin) into the state-maintained sector. It was agreed that the College would serve as a local hub in order to provide a springboard to relaunch classical provision in Blackpool and the surrounding area. Following presentations to several local headteachers' groups, a pilot programme was agreed to be trialled at St. John's Catholic Primary School in nearby Poulton. Although just outside of the Blackpool boundary, the pilot programme provided a valuable opportunity to study the effectiveness of the implementation of Latin as part of the curriculum at Key Stage Two; the feasibility of providing high-quality, efficient and responsive Continuing Professional Development (CPD) for teachers; and, more importantly in light of the challenges faced by so many Blackpool pupils on a daily basis, the link between Latin exposure and development of English academic vocabulary skills. The experience gained from the pilot study at St. John's has been beneficial in making the argument for the inclusion of ancient languages as

32 Peter Wright

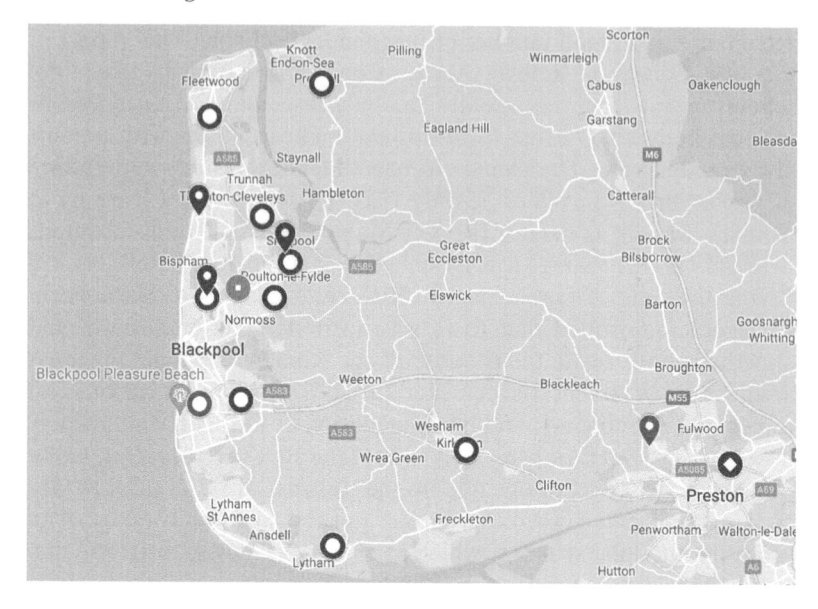

Map 2.1 Locations of educational institutions providing Latin teaching in Blackpool and the surrounding area.

valuable tools to drive effective literacy strategies as part of school improvement. This has resulted in the further expansion of the hub to include additional primary schools, high schools and, perhaps surprisingly, a Pupil Referral Unit (PRU).[2] The notion that the opportunity to study Latin can be seen as desirable, relevant and useful in contexts, which are often unfairly viewed as the most challenging, is especially important. Expanding Classics to twenty-first-century classrooms has been a gradual and organic process.

Map 2.1 shows the locations of educational institutions providing Latin teaching in Blackpool and the surrounding area as part of the Classics for All project. Dark pins with the small circle point to primary schools, white and black round spots point to secondary schools, the lighter grey spot to the Blackpool Sixth Form College and the diamond-shaped spot to Larches High School (PRU).

The motivation for schools to introduce Latin was threefold: (1) to improve academic vocabulary, (2) to widen super-curricular reading and (3) to foster independent learning strategies.

Overcoming barriers to learning

Quigley (2018) highlighted the crucial importance of continuing vocabulary development for all students, of all abilities, in all stages of their education. This is particularly important in an area of high socio-economic disadvantage such as Blackpool since 'limited vocabulary is inextricably linked to a child's home postcode' (Quigley 2018, 4). This awareness of the range of barriers that many children face on a daily basis is absolutely crucial in making the case for the expansion of Classics, in particular Latin, as a highly valuable tool to combat the effects of social and economic disadvantage upon learners. Including Classics in the curriculum can improve learners' confidence in decoding academic vocabulary. The strong relationship between Latin and the language of the academic world means that many students are able to 'decode' some word meanings on first sight via cognates. There is a rich environment for exploring drama, tragedy, myths and stories via role-play, hence providing scope for oracy development, and, crucially for many children, the importance of grammar within language learning provides a valuable opportunity to further reinforce and reiterate English grammatical understanding. For these reasons, teaching Latin provides excellent preparation for SATs.[3] Teachers say that there are cross-curricular benefits: it helps with the teaching of history, it promotes discussions surrounding citizenship and gender, and it provides a platform for investigations into related subject areas; from art to music to drama.

Furthermore, the fact that many Latin courses are narrative-based further boosts their effectiveness within the learning process. This is underlined by Willingham who stated that stories are 'psychologically privileged' in the human mind; that is, there are inherent benefits to students in hanging learning on the coat-peg of story (2009, 66). Similarly, Quigley asserts that 'when explanations of difficult academic concepts ... are clothed with rich linguistic history ... we offer our students a deeper understanding ... they begin to unlock a powerful armoury of tools for reading independently' (2018, 52). While the story of a family from Vindolanda in the *Minimus* Latin course (Bell 1999) (with supporting roles for a charming mouse and mischievous cat) might, at first, seem rather whimsical, this narrative approach to language learning provides pupils with a gradual drip-feed of vocabulary exposure and grammatical development. It is also an accessible, structured and interesting resource which can be delivered effectively by non-specialist teachers.

It is precisely this key benefit which has enabled Latin in Blackpool and the surrounding area to be incorporated into the curriculum by primary schools, secondary academies and a PRU. Through effective and efficient CPD, even teachers with little or no understanding of any modern foreign language (MFL) can be provided with the knowledge and tools to begin a school's journey towards introducing Classics and

Latin. This is important for school leaders with stretched budgets and limited CPD time to offer their staff, and where the problem of recruiting Latin and Classics teachers in an area with little history of such an offer is obvious. One of the key foundation stones for the reintroduction of Latin in any area is the provision of a 'pick up and play' approach from the various courses and resources on offer. Effective resources need to not only inspire pupils but also need to provide a highly structured walkthrough for the novice teacher, including a rich menu of links, activities and resources. Barbara Bell's (1999) *Minimus* course does this and the increasingly confident teacher can find ample opportunities to further explore the themes and myths through various online platforms.

Introducing Latin to a Pupil Referral Unit

The advantages of high-level vocabulary exposure and the development of etymological decoding skills are key reasons why Latin has been introduced by a local state-maintained alternative provision school, Larches High School. Larches is an example of a PRU, sometimes known as a Short Stay School, an educational setting which caters for children who are unable to attend mainstream school for a range of reasons, such as illness or exclusion. These schools are regularly depicted in the press as 'dumping grounds' for disadvantaged learners (Welham 2014), yet pupils experience a very similar set of literacy and vocabulary barriers to their counterparts accessing school in areas of socio-economic disadvantage. Complex terminology is often tricky to understand, lengthy text is difficult to navigate fluently and pupils' speed of reading and comprehension may differ significantly across a teaching group. These barriers have often been exacerbated through non-attendance, home-life issues or lack of effective support at high school and, as a result, teachers look for highly effective methods in order to quickly and efficiently rebuild educational foundations, address learning gaps and promote self-confidence, independence and enthusiasm in students who have had less-than-ideal educational experiences.

Recognising the possible benefits of Latin for their pupils, the leadership team and teachers at this Preston-based referral unit have successfully introduced Latin into the school's curriculum after a trial at Key Stage Three. The school, which has 145 pupils, 55 per cent of whom are in receipt of Free School Meals and 69 per cent of whom qualify for the Pupil Premium (funding granted to schools to improve educational outcomes for disadvantaged pupils), has noted that the exposure to Latin has offered an alternative teaching method which allows pupils to consolidate their understanding of grammar. Such was the enthusiasm from the teaching staff and the pupils for Latin that, during the Covid-19 pandemic and the first national lockdown in March 2020, the school continued to deliver online Latin classes on a weekly basis for pupils. This is perhaps the only PRU in the UK (to the author's knowledge) to deliver Latin in this context.

Supporting teachers to introduce Latin and Classics

Latin has thrived in Blackpool schools as a direct result of effective teacher support sessions. These have taken multiple formats: whole-staff presentations; CPD day courses for non-specialist teachers delivering Latin or Classics for the first time; regular reflection and collaboration sessions between teachers; and the delivery of 'Latin links' workshops as part of the Fylde Coast School Centred Initial Teacher Training (SCITT) programme. In all cases, one of the fundamental pillars of delivery has been to demystify Classics and to dismiss the associated stereotypes of the subject, in all its various forms, as only suitable for the most capable students, irrelevant to education in the twenty-first century, and only accessible to very wealthy students in the independent sector.

One of the easiest (and most effective) ways to achieve this was to illustrate the links to Latin and Ancient Greek within the local environment and common lexicon. From football club slogans to school mottoes, from Nike to the Olympic Games, and from ambulances to politics, teachers became aware that they are actually surrounded by links to the classical world on a daily basis. Moreover, even in the architecture of Victorian Blackpool, a very definite nod to the classical past can be easily viewed on the town's cenotaph, the beautiful Grand Theatre and the (sadly closed) Post Office. Following this discussion, it has been absolutely vital to highlight the importance of the links between Latin and the academic vocabulary used in classrooms and the type of language required in formal academic writing. Certainly, a particularly useful starting activity focused on teachers researching the etymology of many of the subjects offered by their own schools; indeed, many were surprised as to the Latinate origins of the humble tick on a piece of marked work, the ampersand and the symbol for the British Pound. To provide examples of the pedagogical approach used in these sessions, we worked through a common piece of text with which the teachers were highly familiar, such as the school's mission statement or website welcome message, identifying word roots. A recurring theme was that more complex vocabulary nearly always stemmed from Latin or Ancient Greek.

Ancient and modern languages: curricular collaboration?

The inclusion of ancient languages in the Key Stage Two Languages curriculum in 2014 has given Latin and Ancient Greek a 'foot in the door'. However, some leaders and teachers have expressed a concern that choosing to offer Latin or Ancient Greek in place of one of the more commonly delivered modern language trio of French, Spanish or German will place students at a disadvantage when commencing high school. A strength of many of the available approaches and resources for Latin is a focus on developing grammatical understanding from the start, rather than concentrating solely upon the acquisition of vocabulary. As many experienced MFL teachers testify, one of the fundamental aspects of communication is an understanding of the grammatical mechanics of the language being learned. The majority of teachers trained in Blackpool had little or no experience of any MFL – 29 out of 31 teachers attending CPD sessions had not studied a language other than English to GCSE level. Demonstrating that children being introduced to verb conjugation and tenses in Latin early in their school journey provided them with the skills to navigate Key Stage Three French, for example, was useful in reassuring teachers. This was further underlined when one of the highest performing local high schools, St Aidan's, decided to offer Latin through its MFL department. The knowledge and experience of local MFL teams have been especially important in making the case for primary Latin. Indeed, very often, they have been the most vocal of supporters as the enjoyment of, and engagement with, ancient languages at primary level can be an important influence in opting to take a modern language at GCSE level. At a time when the numbers studying GCSE modern languages are a cause for concern nationally (British Council 2022), this is to be celebrated.

What impact has Latin had on young people in Blackpool?

Despite the clear rise in the number of pupils studying Latin in Blackpool schools – with more than 1000 students involved in the subject each week (a figure set to almost double in the next 12 months) – as a result of the establishment of the Blackpool Classics for All Hub, there lingered the crucial question of what impact does the teaching of Latin have on Blackpool school pupils? A vast range of anecdotal evidence certainly suggested that the introduction of Latin and classical subjects was popular and enjoyed in the schools, from enthused teachers and leaders to photographs of pupils performing Latin plays for parents (Newsroom 2019; Gavell 2022) and taking part in various class activities. However, the key issue remained as to whether Latin, in particular, succeeded in boosting English vocabulary acquisition, reinforcing and strengthening English grammatical understanding, and raising achievements of typically under-performing cohorts.

An occasion to investigate this issue presented itself with the implementation of the government's Opportunity Area programme.[4] This government-led strategy focused on helping children in areas of high social and economic deprivation overcome barriers to social mobility. In particular, the establishment of the Blackpool Opportunity Area fund looked to engage practitioners in conducting research as to which methods and pedagogies were effective. The research question 'What impact does the teaching of Latin have on vocabulary development for Year Six pupils?' was decided upon as it would allow for tracking the achievement of over 160 Year Six pupils as they prepared for their SATs. Of the 160, 26 per cent qualified for the Pupil Premium. Another local school agreed to their Year Six cohort being used as a control group. The control group pupils were not exposed to any Latin teaching during the study. The control school had a very similar level of children who qualified for the Pupil Premium, which was important when analysing the results. Finally, all children at the schools involved in the research had no prior formal Latin education.

As the schools involved were using the *Minimus* (Bell 1999) course to deliver the Latin, it was decided to focus the research upon words encountered in *Minimus* which linked to words included in the Tier Two of the Academic Word List (Coxhead 2000). As identified by writers such as Lemov et al. (2016) and Quigley (2018), the teaching of Tier Two words is often the most problematic for teachers and pupils alike. Tier One features high-frequency words that populate spoken language, while Tier Three is characterised by more subject-specific language that can be evidenced within the dialogue of an average Key Stage Three Science classroom. Teachers have developed a range of strategies for the learning and application of Tier Three words, with, anecdotally, an increasing use of etymology evident in many classrooms. Tier Two words, however, typify the language encountered within academic spoken language, texts and exam questions. It is these words that are often barriers to pupil progress.

Minimus 'Starting Out in Latin' (Bell 1999) features 17 of these words – commodity, consume, consumer, duration, facilitate, labour, legislate, maximum, military, minimum, proceed, significant, signify, subordinate, valid, variable and via – which all have some derivation from a Latin word found in the text. The research project aimed to investigate two key issues: firstly, did the students understand the meaning of the Latin words they had been taught? Could they recall and explain the meaning of the words encountered? Secondly, did their understanding of the Latin words mean they were then able to understand the English derivations with greater confidence and reliability? Could the pupils link the Latin word to the English word and understand some basic morphology regarding the relationship between the two words?

As some of the teachers were delivering *Minimus* for the first time, a Latin training day for staff involved in the project was organised. This provided an introduction to the study of Latin and the clear links to English as well as MFL languages such as Spanish, French and Italian. The training day included language learning for staff covering the fundamentals of Latin nouns, adjectives and verbs (including the basics of tenses encountered within the course). The session also included various teaching resources and a suggested scheme of learning to follow. Activities to further develop pupil oracy skills and maintain engagement were shared too. A particularly supportive link was made with Dr Matthew Fitzjohn at the University of Liverpool who included the Blackpool primary schools within the 'Grand Designs in Ancient Greece' project – a programme that uses Lego to provide pupils with interactive archaeology lessons. Indeed, the half-termly use of the Lego with the various archaeology lessons designed by Dr Fitzjohn has become extremely popular with teachers and pupils. Moreover, the use of the Lego has provided an unexpected platform for developing pupil oracy skills via presentations and group collaboration. Finally, staff were provided with three after-school CPD sessions which centred on an exploration and practical use of etymology and morphology within classroom teaching. Once again, an important point to underline is that none of the teachers or classroom assistants involved had ever studied or taught Latin.

Following the training day, an initial baseline assessment was conducted. The four participating teachers followed the agreed Blackpool Latin scheme of learning. The teachers varied in their level of experience (one classroom assistant, two teachers with more than five years' experience and one recently qualified teacher). Latin lessons consisted of 45-minute sessions for all pupils, regardless of ability or prior attainment. The data collected from the baseline test and final assessment has been eye-opening. Despite the teaching being curtailed by the Covid-19 pandemic at, roughly, the halfway stage of the academic year, the progress of pupils involved has revealed significant progress made by boys. Overall, 73 per cent of males involved in the project improved their understanding of the Latin words selected and the link to the English Tier Two words derived from the Latin. Pupils were tested in their knowledge of the Latin words encountered (through matching translation tasks) but, crucially, in their ability to match definitions of the English word derived from the Latin. Overall, 64 per cent of females saw an improvement in the accuracy of their understanding of the Tier Two English words and 56 per cent of children who qualify as Pupil Premium recipients improved their scores on average by 25 per cent. It is clear that just 45 minutes of Latin per week over 17 weeks has had substantial vocabulary benefits for pupils. These small-scale research findings indicate that there is a positive correlation between learning Latin and pupil understanding of English vocabulary with Latinate roots. Further research is needed to understand the mechanisms behind this improvement and to optimise teaching and learning approaches.

The successful expansion of Latin to an area that has no recent history of classical provision and has so many socio-economic challenges is a powerful message. For too long, Classics has been limited to the independent sector or state schools in leafy suburbia. However, it is students in towns such as Blackpool who stand to gain the most from a reintroduction of Classics in the non-selective state sector. The Blackpool project has shown that pupils, parents, teachers and leaders reacted positively to the reintroduction of Latin. Crucially, for school leaders with stretched budgets, the introduction of Latin and Classics is cost-effective. It is important that the findings and evidence of the Blackpool schools is viewed within the economically restrictive context in which all educators currently operate. Latin has been successfully delivered, in Blackpool schools, by teachers or teaching assistants with no prior knowledge of the language. Training events (financed by the Opportunity Area fund) took just 15 hours (on average) of the CPD allowance of an individual teacher, and once the initial outlay on teaching resources had been taken into account, there was minimal further cost to schools.

Which resources and support have made this possible?

Organisations and charities such as Advocating Classics Education (ACE), the Classical Association and Classics for All have done a fantastic job in raising awareness of the benefits of Latin, Ancient Greek, Classical Civilisation and Ancient History for learners from primary school through to A-Level and beyond. As a result, there is a range of courses and resources available for schools seeking to introduce Classics. Blackpool schools have used a mixture of these courses, to suit individual school contexts and priorities. The vast majority of participating Blackpool primaries have been using the well-established and highly popular *Minimus* course, published by Cambridge University Press (Bell 1999). This course provides students with an opportunity to learn basic Latin vocabulary and grammar, and gives an introduction to Roman Britain, with well-structured resources and lesson plans that are accessible even to the busiest of teachers. The *Minimus* offer is further complemented by online resources, and the learning is developed further by the *Minimus Secundus* course. Primarily, training days focused on the *Minimus* Latin course, but this was supplemented by Classics for All's *Maximum Classics* and *Mega Greek* courses for schools. These free and ready-to-use resources were often the stimuli for schools deciding to offer Latin more formally on the curriculum. Additionally, two welcome newcomers have further buoyed the traditional offering of the tried-and-tested Cambridge Latin course: Hands Up Education's *Suburani* course and Classics for All's *Basil Batrakhos* course have engaged students and teachers with new approaches and content.

Conclusion

Latin has had, and continues to have, positive benefits for pupils in Blackpool and surrounding areas. Firstly, the relationship between the study of Latin and improved English literacy is increasingly being investigated, while the potential of Latin to boost engagement for boys is exciting. This is an area which is ripe for further research in order to clarify why Latin seems to have such an impact on the vocabulary achievement of boys in Blackpool, and if this is replicated in other educational contexts.

Secondly, the successful expansion of Latin into a PRU as part of the school's literacy plan illustrates how the dominant narrative about what Classics is, and whom it is for, is changing. Furthermore, this highlights how Latin can reinforce and strengthen vocabulary acquisition approaches for all pupils, even those who might be labelled 'hardest to reach'.

Finally, given the clear evidence in Blackpool that Latin can be successfully delivered by non-specialist teachers (with a little training) and is cost-effective, the question about the relevance of Latin in a twenty-first-century UK classroom evolves from 'Why should schools teach Latin?' to 'Why aren't all schools teaching Latin?'.

Notes

1 From 2009 to 2016. The A-level reforms affecting entry from 2015/2016 have resulted in students, on the whole, selecting only three A Level choices, rather than the standard four choices for the now defunct AS/A2. This

has led to a decline in numbers. However, in comparison to many areas, recruitment continues to be positive for A-Level Ancient History with over 110 learners studying the course over Years 12 and 13 (ages 16–18).
2 A Pupil Referral Unit is an alternative education provision for students unable to access mainstream school for a range of reasons, from exclusions to special educational needs.
3 SATs (Standard Assessment Tests) measure student achievement in maths and reading at the end of Key Stage One (Year Two – age seven) and the end of Key Stage Two (Year Six – age 11) in English schools.
4 Opportunity Areas are a government initiative to raise education standards in areas of low achievement. Blackpool was identified as one of these areas. This resulted in a £10,000 grant from the Opportunity Area to support Latin teaching in Blackpool and local research to identify the impact(s) of Latin learning on pupils.

Reference List

Bell, B. 1999. *Minimus: Starting out in Latin.* Cambridge: Cambridge University Press.

British Council. 2022. *Languages Trends 2022: Language Teaching in primary and secondary schools in England.* London: British Council. Accessed 27 July 2022. https://www.britishcouncil.org/sites/default/files/language_trends_report_2022.pdf.

Coxhead, A. (2000). "Academic Word List sublist families". Accessed 31 October 2021. https://www.wgtn.ac.nz/lals/resources/academicwordlist/sublist.

Gavell, T. 2022. "When in Rome – the Blackpool pupils lapping up Latin lessons". *Blackpool Gazette*, 3 May. Accessed 27 July 2022. https://www.blackpoolgazette.co.uk/education/when-in-rome-the-blackpool-pupils-lapping-up-latin-lessons-3678800.

Lemov, D., C. Driggs and E. Woolway. 2016. *Reading Reconsidered: Rigorous Literacy Instruction.* San Francisco: Jossey-Bass.

Ministry of Housing, Communities and Local Government. 2019. "The English Indices of Deprivation". Accessed 23 June 2021. https://assets.publishing.service.gov.uk/government/uploads/system/uploads/attachment_data/file/835115/IoD2019_Statistical_Release.pdf.

Newsroom. 2019. "How Latin is making a comeback in Fylde coast schools". *Blackpool Gazette*, 30 January. Accessed 27 July 2022. https://www.blackpoolgazette.co.uk/education/how-latin-making-comeback-fylde-coast-schools-144610.

Quigley, A. 2018. *Closing the Vocabulary Gap.* London: Routledge.

Welham, H. 2014. "Pupil referral units a 'dumping ground'". *The Guardian*, 16 May. Accessed 27 July 2022. https://www.theguardian.com/teacher-network/teacher-blog/2014/may/16/pupil-referral-units-sats-teaching-education-round-up.

Willingham, D. 2009. *Why Don't Students Like School? A cognitive scientist answers questions about how the mind works and what it means for the classroom.* San Francisco: Jossey-Bass.

3 Using classical mythology to teach English as an Additional Language

Anna Bloor, Meghan McCabe and Arlene Holmes-Henderson

Introduction

The study of classical mythology in English translation is interesting, rich and complex. Its themes go to the very core of the human condition and include metamorphosis, war, revenge, rage and divine punishment. Despite being thousands of years old, these stories have an enduring power that engages contemporary audiences, young and old. For decades, in British schools, classical subjects have largely been the preserve of the intellectual and/or the financial elite. The seven per cent of the population who attend fee-paying schools have reasonable access to the study of classical mythology, ancient world studies and perhaps also Latin (Holmes-Henderson 2017; Hunt and Holmes-Henderson 2021). The 93 per cent of the population who attend non-fee-paying schools have patchy access to the study of classical subjects. This chapter showcases the introduction of classical mythology as a unit within the English subject curriculum at Key Stage Three (KS3) and presents findings which indicate particular benefit for newly arrived refugee students learning English as an Additional Language (EAL).

School context

The Bemrose School, an all-through school situated in Derby, undertook – and continues to run – a mythology project in the secondary phase. Although the local area does not fall into the highly deprived category, Derby City Council (2020) reported that it has a slightly higher percentage of children in absolute low-income (18.2 per cent) and relative low-income (22 per cent) households than the national average (15.3 per cent and 18.4 per cent, respectively). The school has approximately 1000 students aged 11–16 on roll, with over 50 per cent of those speaking EAL – a much higher percentage than the national

DOI: 10.4324/9781003181958-4

average of 17.1 per cent (Department for Education 2020). The first languages spoken by the students include Urdu, Romanian and Italian, with a large percentage of the cohort speaking Romani alongside some Slovak. In Key Stage Three (KS3), small groups of EAL students who are not yet able to access the National Curriculum are given a bespoke timetable, which includes many of the same lessons as their non-EAL peers but with additional English and Maths lessons to help them gain core knowledge and skills. Students who are new to the country attend the Welcome Group in order to learn the basic language they will need to participate in mainstream lessons.

The Roma-Slovak community has a high level of mobility, and many students therefore leave and rejoin the school at different points throughout the academic year. Gould (2017) notes that some Gypsy Roma Traveller (GRT) communities feel that formal education is not a key aspect of their lives, which could account for variation in attendance. Furthermore, many Roma-Slovak families settle in different countries and therefore take time out of the school year to visit relatives. Due to the mobility of the Roma-Slovak students between different countries, the EAL groups frequently change in terms of numbers, first languages spoken, ability in English and behavioural dynamics. Although the range of languages spoken adds a diversity of cultures and perspectives, which enriches the educational experiences of all students and the teachers, the non-standard and non-literary nature of the Romani language can result in difficulty with 'linguistic integration' (Payne 2016, 10). Many of these students have had periods of no-schooling and, due to the discrimination against the Roma community in Slovakia and other Eastern European countries, several parents fear that their children will face prejudice. This affects the way in which Roma students perceive both their own ability and their experience of the education system (Ofsted 2014).

Underpinning research

The study of literature plays a crucial role in the teaching and learning of the English language at The Bemrose School. The focus on referential texts in qualifications such as Functional Skills in English, amongst others, often encourages the teaching of informational and non-fiction texts. However, these can be limited in terms of vocabulary, syntactical structures and ultimately students often fail to engage (O'Connell 2009). A key focus of the KS3 English National Curriculum is to 'develop the habit of reading widely and often, for both pleasure and information' (Department for Education 2013), which is beneficial for Key Stage 4 (KS4) as it gives students a solid understanding of literature before students embark on the GCSE syllabus. McKeown (2014) notes that, although Functional Skills in English and GCSE English courses have some similarities, the length and complexity of the texts students are exposed to in the GCSE specification, as well as the in-depth analysis required to gain marks, makes the GCSE content more difficult than that of the Functional English course.

Daskalovska and Dimova (2012) suggest that the use of authentic texts such as newspaper articles, maps and advertisements does not allow students to explore beyond the referential function of language and may limit their own expression. It is argued, instead, that the representational language offered by literary texts allows students to engage with stories that not only spark creativity but also make use of unusual and unexpected uses of language; metaphors, idioms, puns and proverbs, in a way that referential materials may not (Daskalovska and Dimova 2012). The appealing narrative of literature often helps embed the language within the learner's memory even if some words are not understood. Hoque (2007) reinforces the idea that vocabulary teaching relies heavily on context and that students often use contextual clues in stories to work out the meaning of words they have not previously encountered. Data collected by Demie (2012) suggests that it can take EAL learners five to seven years to obtain academic English proficiency, which further emphasises the importance of exposing students to as broad a range of complex vocabulary and texts as possible.

In order to expose students to a wide range of literary texts while improving cultural capital from the start of their secondary school experience, in 2019 the English Department at The Bemrose School reorganised and diversified the Year Seven curriculum to include the study of Greek mythology. The reasons for implementing Greek mythology into the curriculum, alongside key religious stories, folktales and legends across countries and cultures, were multiple. Firstly, the use of traditional tales such as mythology and folktales 'belong to the oral tradition of storytelling, passed from generation to generation, often crossing cultures' (Mourão 2009, 19), which allowed links to be explored between the texts and traditions of the oral-based Romani language. The inclusion of a diverse range of stories also ensured the students felt like their cultures were represented. This raised the value of stories and experiences from the students' cultures that may have previously been underrepresented or even misrepresented in the curriculum. The typical structure of traditional stories benefits language learners as they can start to recognise patterns, make predictions and emulate structures in their own creative writing.

Secondly, as mentioned by Dowden (1992), Greek mythology does not exist in isolation and the study of mythology opens up discussion about topics such as morality, the human condition, politics, geography, religion and etymology. From company names such as *Nike* to idiomatic references such as *Achilles' heel, Pandora's box* and *the Trojan horse*, it is easy to make cross-curricular links via Greek mythology (Holmes-Henderson 2021) and exposure to these stories at a young age unlocks meaning in a wide range of situations. An understanding of mythology and its legacy in literature benefits students when they explore many other texts but especially when they study Shakespeare's plays. Although described as having 'small Latin, and less Greek', classical references are peppered throughout many of Shakespeare's plays and poems (Dickson 2016). When students are aware of the stories behind names used by Shakespeare, such as Aurora or Echo, a deeper understanding of the text is unlocked and the complexity of meaning is illuminated.

Additionally, the subjective nature of mythology, like most literature, allows students to relate to the stories and find their own meanings and morals. Although it is not necessary for texts to be relevant for learning to occur, Daskalovska and Dimova (2012) argue that language development relies on active engagement from the students; emotional connections to a text enable students to react and respond creatively themselves. Tigue (1992, 24) notes that mythology is still relevant for students in the twenty-first century as

> 'most human beings may not identify with the role of king or princess, but they do have knowledge of the tasks associated with being a president or corporate executive; money, power, honor, crisis, decisions, manipulation, and kindness were, are, and will be here for a long time'.

At The Bemrose School, Year Seven pupils study Greek Mythology for a whole term, focusing on creative writing skills as they study a number of stories (including the creation myth and stories about the Trojan War). The focus then shifts to inference and analytical skills while studying *The Odyssey*. The content of *The Odyssey* has particular relevance to the context of this school. There are strong parallels between the millions of people seeking refuge due to conflict, discrimination and persecution around the world and the feelings of displacement experienced by Odysseus on his epic journey in search of home (Goble and Wiersum 2019). Studying *The Odyssey* encourages students to consider not only the feelings of isolation and confusion that may be felt by those away from home but also the importance of welcoming and being hospitable to those who are new to a country or place. Aware that this text, and discussion of it, could be triggering for some students and could potentially cause anxiety or upset, teachers completed professional development in trauma-informed pedagogies.

Selecting texts

Choosing an appropriate text for students can be a difficult task, especially when teaching Greek mythology as there are numerous translations and works available. The Bemrose School utilised two versions of *The Odyssey*: the Usborne Young Reading hardcover retold by Louie Stowell and a retelling from Geraldine McCaughrean. The Usborne edition is a simple retelling of *The Odyssey* in a large font and is illustrated with large, colourful pictures throughout the text. As mentioned by Scrivener (2011), illustrations can assist EAL students in making predictions about the text and providing some context and background information. The McCaughrean version, however, is much more complex in terms of vocabulary and syntactic structure and has a standard-sized font and fewer illustrations. Despite, or rather because of, their differences, both texts were utilised in the classroom for a range of differing activities. As stated by Duff and Maley (2007), when simpler texts are used, the teacher can provide complexity through the use of teaching activities and questioning. Similarly, when more complex texts are used, the teacher can scaffold and support the students in understanding the text.

Reading aloud

A motivation for introducing Greek mythology was a departmental strategy to increase the opportunities for teachers to read aloud to their classes. There have been a number of studies that measure how teachers reading aloud to their class impact the comprehension abilities of the students. Westbrook et al. (2018) found that reading challenging novels at a faster pace enabled students to make eight and a half months' progress (on average) on standardised comprehension tests. They also found that the greatest impact was made on students seen as poorer readers, which could be significant for EAL students who often struggle more with comprehending texts in English. Furthermore, Neugebauer and Currie-Robin (2009) discuss the multiple benefits of reading aloud specifically for bilingual students: these include vocabulary development, understanding of literary devices and comprehension. Reading aloud also helps 'students engage in discussions about text and discover word meanings through interactions with peers and teachers' (Neugebauer and Currie-Robin 2009, 396). This idea is unpacked further by O'Connell (2009) as the usual intensive reading undertaken in English lessons accompanied by multiple-choice questions or comprehension activities can limit the opportunities for students to explore their own interpretations. In order to build a 'strong bond' between the student and the text, opportunities need to be given for reading aloud and class discussion (O'Connell 2009, 13). The role of the teacher as an experienced and accomplished reader is imperative as it allows students to focus solely on the plot, characters, symbols, structure and vocabulary as well as sparking an enjoyment of reading and literature. Due to the vast amount of research in this area and the positive impact reading aloud has been shown to have on students, the English Department decided to dedicate more time to the teacher reading aloud in the mythology unit as well as to facilitating activities which promoted student discussion of the texts.

Analysis of practice: what does the teaching of *The Odyssey* look like in The Bemrose School?

Pre-reading, while-reading and post-reading

The lessons for EAL students at The Bemrose School followed a recommended structure for teaching language through the means of reading a text: the 'pre-reading, while-reading and post-reading phases' (Jiraskova 2018, 33). Each part of the teaching structure built on the previous knowledge of the students, who were eventually able to comprehend new vocabulary and grammar in texts subconsciously, therefore building their confidence as independent readers (Scrivener 2011). The text pre-reading phase aimed at encouraging motivation in the students and building suspense into the content of the text (Jiraskova 2018). Often making connections between the students themselves and the topic of the text can be a successful way of encouraging motivation (Scrivener 2011), but with issues such as forced migration, conflict and familial separation, it was vital that teachers approached the reading of *The Odyssey* with trauma-informed pedagogies (Sadin and Levy 2018; Bashant 2020; Brunzell and Norrish 2021). During this stage, students were explicitly taught new Tier Two vocabulary that they would encounter in the text to avoid hindrance to their comprehension (Scrivener 2011). The combination of these approaches to the pre-reading stage was conducive to producing confident readers who 'believed in their reading abilities' (Jiraskova 2018, 34) and who felt safe to participate.

In order to achieve this, a variety of activities were used at The Bemrose School during the pre-reading phase of *The Odyssey*. To pre-teach Tier Two vocabulary, the teacher made selections from the chapter that the students would begin to read in the next lesson and found appropriate images to explain them clearly to the students. A maximum of ten Tier Two words were chosen at a time and placed in a box at the top of a PowerPoint slide. An image which matched one of the chosen words was then placed on the slide; this was then repeated until there were ten slides with individual images on and the ten words at the top. As a class, students were asked to decide which new word matched the image on the screen. Once the class had completed this orally, the teacher put up a slide with all of the numbered images and new vocabulary and asked the students to match them individually in their exercise books.

This activity became a starter activity for the next lesson to help the teacher monitor which vocabulary had been retained by the students. Once this had been completed, students were then provided with gaps in ten sentences that they had to complete with one of the newly acquired words to check that they understood the words in context. This exercise enabled students with EAL to acquire new vocabulary which, in turn, prepared them to demonstrate their understanding of the text. By exposing students with EAL to Tier Two words in this way, the literacy gap between the newcomer group and L1 English students was successfully reduced (activities of this kind and their impacts have been documented elsewhere by Beck et al. 2002).

To encourage motivation and interest in *The Odyssey*, teachers at The Bemrose School also introduced students to the exploration of morphology in the pre-reading phrase. A student with EAL is not going to become competent in the language by simply increasing the number of words they acquire; they also need to be able to comprehend new words through their knowledge of others in the language (Paiman et al. 2015). Many English words are borrowed from other languages, such as Ancient Greek and Latin, which can enable students to observe similarities between English and their home language. This can help to generate interest in the patterns of languages and encourage them to explore this further when approaching unfamiliar words. Being able to use morphemic cues to comprehend the meaning of a word provides students with confidence when faced with unknown complex vocabulary in a text (Varatharajoo et al. 2015).

As a result, English teachers at The Bemrose School provided students with Ancient Greek morphemes that the English language has borrowed over time and which they would encounter in the text of *The Odyssey*. They then examined the etymology of the morphemes with the students to aid them in understanding complex words that utilise them, for example the morpheme 'chrono'. Once students were able to comprehend the meaning of the root word 'chrono' (time) and the Ancient Greek origins in the story of Chronos, the god of time, they could decipher the meanings of more complex vocabulary that used the root word, for example the word 'chronology'. When reading *The Odyssey*, the students used morphological cues from words they already knew to help them to decode new vocabulary. This encouraged students to continue reading when they came across a word they were unfamiliar with; they used both their morphemic cues and the context of the unfamiliar word with regard to the surrounding words to comprehend the text, therefore increasing their reading assurance.

Once students built their confidence and their vocabulary knowledge, teaching moved on to the while-reading stage. Comprehension is at the centre of the while-reading stage and can take the form of either comprehension of the structure of the language used in the text, or comprehension of the themes, symbols and the author's intention (Jiraskova 2018). Comprehension of the language does not simply mean understanding the referential language used in the text, for example *a dark sky means that the weather is bad*, it also refers to exploring the representational language used in a text that requires the student to engage their imagination to fully comprehend it, for example *a dark sky can signal foreboding in literature* (McRae 1991). By exploring the representational language in a text, students can engage with it on a deeper level through the connections to their emotions and empathy, therefore deepening their understanding (O'Connell 2009). In order to achieve this deeper connection with *The Odyssey*, teachers at The Bemrose School utilised the process of reciprocal reading. To understand a new text, students needed to be able to draw on their 'language skills, relevant background knowledge, and ability to infer', all of which are utilised in the reciprocal reading process (Quigley and Coleman 2019, 15).

Reciprocal reading

Reciprocal reading is composed of four stages: prediction, clarifying, questioning and summarising (Quigley and Coleman 2019). Through this process, students develop a deeper knowledge of the representational language of the text. They identify the themes and symbols, by making their own observations before reading and monitoring these while reading, clarifying words and phrases that they are unfamiliar with, and questioning the ideas of the text. Finally, they summarise the content and meaning of the text to enable the teacher to assess their success in comprehension (Quigley and Coleman 2019). To provide an example, a teacher at The Bemrose School looked at the following extract from *The Odyssey* when completing the reciprocal reading process:

> 'A breeze sprang up. The breezes braided themselves into a wind. The wind twisted itself into a gusting gale and the gale screwed itself into a frenzy' (McCaughrean 1993, 4).

The students had the verb 'braided' and the noun 'frenzy' explained to them by the teacher during the pre-reading process to enable them to clarify their understanding of the image being described. They were then asked what they could infer about the weather from the verbs 'sprang' and 'screwed'. To summarise their understanding of the image, they made a quick illustration of how this image looked in their own mind. This process of reciprocal reading enables students to comprehend the 'meanings of codes and signs that are dictated by culture and society' (Goh 1986, 2) and found in texts such as *The Odyssey*.

Teachers at The Bemrose School helped students to learn about the author's intention by extracting quotations from *The Odyssey* linked to the character of Odysseus and asking students to consider what the language showed about his character. This approach encouraged students to share their different responses to the text, involved them in the process of critical thinking, making them aware of the cultural representations of the language used in the text (Ferradas 2009). By doing so, the students accessed another level of comprehension of the vocabulary in *The Odyssey* and the author's thought process behind the words chosen, in addition to comprehending the language used. This practice allowed them to further develop both their speaking and reading skills (Jiraskova 2018).

The post-reading phase of the text encouraged students to review their learning, respond to what they have learned, as well as providing an opportunity for pupils to adapt the text themselves, therefore demonstrating the extent to which they have engaged with the text and understood the levels of language used within it (Scrivener 2011). Students are now at a point in their learning where they have acquired new knowledge, but something must be done with this knowledge to ensure that they can adapt it and apply their knowledge to later learning (Wahjudi 2010). Open questions that invited discussion and interpretation were used in the English learner classrooms at The Bemrose

School to attain this response to the text (Bleiman 2020). Examples of these questions included: *what's your favourite moment in the text? Find a place where you felt tense. Find an example of something unexpected. Why is so much of the extract about Odysseus' pride? What impression do you have of Penelope? How have you got that impression?* Bleiman (2020) suggests that discussion between students similar to the questions demonstrated above can not only extend their knowledge and understanding of the text but also encourages pupils to alter their way of thinking about the text, and therefore their knowledge, due to their interaction with other students' interpretations.

Discussion also helps the students to use the reading skills they have developed while improving speaking, listening and writing (Saricoban 2002). This was further accomplished by the teachers providing the students with statements about *The Odyssey*; the students were asked to decide which were the most interesting or the most important and to expand on their reasons for this in a class discussion (Bleiman 2020). Examples of the statements provided were: *Odysseus is a flawed hero; the female characters of the epic are more powerful than the men; Penelope is just as guilty as Odysseus for the deaths of the maids.* These statements required students to both practise and summarise the critical thinking they had used previously when reading the text and reach a firm opinion about what they had studied (Ferradas 2009). The statements also allowed the students to return to the keywords they had previously studied in the pre-reading stage and demonstrate their new understanding by adapting them to fit the context of their personal response sentences (Khamraeva 2016).

Conclusion

The success of teaching Greek mythology to KS3 EAL classes at The Bemrose School was evident through the requests of multiple students to read the story of *The Iliad* after it was referred to during lessons on *The Odyssey*. Enjoyment, rather than fear, was the prevailing attitude of students towards Greek mythology. Class teachers commented on their students' increased motivation and enjoyment of reading Greek mythology aloud as the lessons developed, and they became more familiar with the vocabulary through their morphology lessons. One class teacher commented on the enthusiasm of a student when researching the etymology of one word and being able to explain how it linked to Slovak, their own first language. Making these connections appeared to increase students' confidence as Greek mythology no longer seemed to be something that was only accessible to others but was for their enjoyment too. Later in the school year, students were exposed to both Shakespearean and Biblical stories which they appeared to navigate with confidence due to the many shared allusions from Greek mythology (Dickson 2016). Members of the senior leadership team commented on the impressive use of Tier Two vocabulary used in the students' creative writing, using their work as examples to inform the expectations of language learners across the school.

Resulting from the success of this project, a proposal was advanced to increase the amount of time allocated to reading for pleasure in English lessons. A project is now being started in which all English classes at The Bemrose School, including EAL classes, will be read to by their teacher during one lesson a week. The book choice will be the individual teacher's personal preference which they think will engage pupils and encourage them to develop a joy of reading. This is aimed at discovering whether the benefits of this project would be achieved by reading a variety of fiction with students or whether there was something uniquely valuable about Greek mythology. The Bemrose School project shows that classical mythology can be an effective tool for helping students with EAL engage with representational language, acquire Tier Two vocabulary and utilise morphemic cues learned in the pre-reading phase when in the while-reading phase. *The Odyssey* was an appropriate choice of text which offered excellent opportunities for reading aloud, reciprocal reading, and developing additional skills in speaking, listening and writing, all of which contribute to pupils' improved confidence and proficiency in English. Staff have required minimal additional training, and the resources required for the unit have been low cost. Based on our experience, we encourage English teachers and inclusion specialists in other settings to expand their practice and embark on their own journey with *The Odyssey*.

Reference List

Bashant, J. 2020. *Building a Trauma-Informed, Compassionate Classroom: Strategies & Activities to Reduce Challenging Behavior, Improve Learning Outcomes, and Increase Student Engagement.* Eau Claire: PESI Publishing.

Beck, I., M. G. McKeown and L. Kucan. 2002. *Bringing words to life: Robust vocabulary instruction: Solving problems in the teaching of literacy.* New York: Guilford Press.

Bleiman, B. 2020. *What Matters in English Teaching.* London: English and Media Centre.

Brunzell, T. and J. Norrish. 2021. *Creating Trauma-Informed, Strengths-Based Classrooms: Teacher Strategies for Nurturing Students' Healing, Growth, and Learning.* London: Jessica Kingsley Publishers.

Daskalovska, N. and N. Dimova. 2012. "Why should Literature be Used in the Language Classroom?". *Procedia – Social and Behavioral Sciences* 46: 1182–1186. Accessed 12 November 2020. https://doi.org/10.1016/j.sbspro.2012.05.271.

Demie, F. 2012. "English as an additional language pupils: How long does it take to acquire English fluency?" *Language and Education* 27 (1): 59–69. Accessed 12 November 2020. https://doi.org/10.1080/09500782.2012.682580.

Department for Education. 2013. "English programmes of study: key stage 3. National curriculum in England". Accessed 12 November 2020. https://assets.publishing.service.gov.uk/government/uploads/system/uploads/attachment_data/file/244215/SECONDARY_national_curriculum_-_English2.pdf.

Department for Education. 2020. "Schools, pupils and their characteristics". Accessed 10 February 2021. https://explore-education-statistics.service.gov.uk/find-statistics/school-pupils-and-their-characteristics.

Derby City Council. 2020. "Info4Derby: Deprivation". Accessed 12 November 2020. https://info4derby.derby.gov.uk/deprivation/.

Dickson, A. 2016. "What the Romans did for Shakespeare: Rome and Roman values in Shakespeare's plays". *The British Library*. Accessed 10 February 2021. https://www.bl.uk/shakespeare/articles/what-the-romans-did-for-shakespeare-rome-and-roman-values-in-shakespeares-plays.

Dowden, K. 1992. *The Uses of Greek Mythology*. London: Routledge.

Duff, A. and A. Maley. 2007. *Literature* (Resource Books for Teachers). Oxford: Oxford University Press.

Ferradas, C. 2009. "Enjoying literature with teens and young adults in the English language class." In *BritLit: Using Literature in EFL Classrooms*, edited by F. O'Connell, 27–31. London: British Council. Accessed 9 February 2021. https://www.teachingenglish.org.uk/sites/teacheng/files/pub_BritLit_elt.pdf.

Goble, R. and E. Wiersum. 2019. "Epic explorations: Teaching the 'Odyssey' with The New York Times." *The New York Times*. Accessed 23 September 2020. https://www.nytimes.com/2019/03/21/learning/lesson-plans/epic-explorations-teaching-the-odyssey-with-the-new-york-times.html.

Goh, L. 1986. *Using Myth, Folktales and Fairytales in the Adult ESL Classroom*. University of British Columbia: Faculty of Education.

Gould, S. 2017. "Promoting the social inclusion and academic progress of Gypsy, Roma and Traveller children: a secondary school case study." *Educational Psychology in Practice* 33 (2): 126–148. Accessed 23 September 2020. https://doi.org/10.1080/02667363.2016.1259996.

Holmes-Henderson, A. 2017. "Classical subjects in schools: A comparative study of New Zealand and the United Kingdom". In *Athens to Aotearoa: Greece and Rome in New Zealand Literature and Society*, edited by D. Burton, S. Perris and J. Tatum, 326–346. Victoria: University Wellington Press.

Holmes-Henderson, A. 2021. "Developing multiliteracies through classical mythology in British classrooms". In *Our Mythical Education: The Reception of Classical Myth Worldwide in Formal Education, 1900–2020*, edited by L. Maurice, 139–151. Warsaw: Warsaw University Press.

Hoque, E. 2007. "The Use of Literature in Teaching English as a Foreign Language (TEFL)". *Harvest Jahangirnagar Studies of Literature and Language* 22. Accessed 23 September 2020. https://www.academia.edu/33316043/The_Use_of_Literature_in_Teaching_English_as_a_Foreign_Language.

Hunt, S. and A. Holmes-Henderson. 2021. "A level Classics poverty. Classical subjects in schools in England: access, attainment and progression". *CUCD Bulletin* 50: 1–26. Accessed 13 September 2021. https://cucd.blogs.sas.ac.uk/files/2021/02/Holmes-Henderson-and-Hunt-Classics-Poverty.docx.pdf.

Jiraskova, A. 2018. *Teaching English Through Literature at Secondary Schools*. Masaryk University, Faculty of Arts, 6–144. Accessed 23 September 2020. https://is.muni.cz/th/a4lvs/Diplomova_prace_finfin_Jiraskova.pdf.

Khamraeva, G. I. 2016. "Benefits of implementation of pre-, while and post reading activities in language learning." *International Scientific Journal* 4 (1): 45–46.

McCaughrean, G. 1993. *The Odyssey: Retold*. London: Penguin Random House.

McKeown, A. 2014. "From teaching ESOL to GCSE English." *Language Issues* 25: 30–33. Accessed 13 September 2021. http://natecla.org.uk/uploads/media/208/16341.pdf.

McRae, J. 1991. *Literature with a Small "l"*. London and Basingstoke: Macmillan.

Mourão, S. 2009. "Using stories in the primary classroom." In *BritLit: Using Literature in EFL Classrooms*, edited by F. O'Connell, 17–26. London: British Council. Accessed 23 September 2020. https://www.teachingenglish.org.uk/sites/teacheng/files/pub_BritLit_elt.pdf.

Neugebauer, S. R. and R. Currie-Robin. 2009. "Read-Alouds in Calca, Peru: A Bilingual Indigenous Context". *The Reading Teacher* 62 (5): 396–405.

O'Connell, F. 2009. "*BritLit: Using Literature in EFL Classrooms*". London: British Council. Accessed 23 September 2020. https://www.teachingenglish.org.uk/sites/teacheng/files/pub_BritLit_elt.pdf.

Ofsted. 2014. "Overcoming barriers: ensuring that Roma children are fully engaged and achieving in education". Accessed 23 September 2020. https://assets.publishing.service.gov.uk/government/uploads/system/uploads/attachment_data/file/430866/Overcoming_barriers_-_ensuring_that_Roma_children_are_fully_engaged_and_achieving_in_education.pdf.

Paiman, N., V. Ngee Thai and C. Mei Yuit. 2015. "Effectiveness of Morphemic Analysis of Graeco-Latin Word Parts as a Vocabulary Learning Strategy among ESL Learners." *The Southeast Asian Journal of English Language Studies*, 21 (2): 31–45. Accessed 23 September 2020. https://doi.org/10.17576/3L-2015-2102-03.

Payne, M. 2016. "The inclusion of Slovak Roma pupils in secondary school: Contexts of language policy and planning." *Current Issues in Language Planning* 18 (2): 161–180. Accessed 24 September 2020. https://doi.org/10.1080/14664208.2016.1220281.

Quigley, A. and R. Coleman. 2019. *Improving Literacy in Secondary Schools: Guidance Report*. Education Endowment Foundation.

Sadin, M. and N. Levy. 2018. *Teachers' Guide to Trauma: 20 Things Kids with Trauma Wish Their Teachers Knew*. New York: Nathan Levy Books.

Saricoban, A. 2002. "Reading Strategies of Successful Readers through the Three Phase Approach". *The Reading Matrix* 2 (3): 1–16.

Scrivener, J. 2011. *Learning Teaching: The Essential Guide to English Language Teaching*, 3rd ed. London: Macmillan.

Tigue, J. W. 1992. "Teaching mythology as a subtext of the humanities". *The Journal of General Education* 41: 23–31.

Varatharajoo, C., A. B. Asmawi, N. Abdallah and M. Abedalaziz. 2015. "Morphemic analysis awareness: impact on ESL students' vocabulary learning strategy". *International Scholarly and Scientific Research & Innovation*, 9: 3263–3269.

Wahjudi, A. 2010. "Interactive post-reading activities that work". *Bahasa dan Seni: Jurnal Bahasa, Sastra, Seni, dan Pengajarannya* 38 (1): 84–92.

Westbrook, J., J. Sutherland, J. Oakhill and S. Sullivan. 2018. "'Just reading': the impact of a faster pace of reading narratives on the comprehension of poorer adolescent readers in English classrooms". *Literacy* 53 (3): 60–68. Accessed 24 September 2020. https://doi.org/10.1111/lit.12141.

4 Student perceptions of BAME people in the Roman world
A comparison of Latin textbooks

Alex Gruar

Introduction

Attention has been drawn to the need for appropriate reflection of Black, Asian and minority ethnic[1] (BAME) people's experiences in curricular materials in the UK, including The Runnymede Trust's 2020 Report 'Race and Racism in English Secondary Schools' (Joseph-Salisbury 2020) and the Council of University Classics Departments' (2020) 'Equality and Diversity in Classics' Report. This scrutiny has been reflected in Classics teaching, with the creation of new resources, for example the Warwick Classics Network's Diversity/BAME Teaching Resources, but there remains tension between the concern that the discipline was historically a gatekeeper for elite, male privilege and the potential opportunities afforded by a subject centred on the Mediterranean, which thus explores not only Europe but also the peoples and civilisations of Africa and Asia.

This research was carried out in a boys' selective school in Buckinghamshire with an increasingly ethnically diverse intake. In the year 2020–2021, 44 per cent of students attending the school were identified by their parents or guardians as BAME, 22 per cent spoke English as an Additional Language and four per cent were in receipt of the Pupil Premium. In September 2020, training was offered to the whole staff on anti-racism, and an Action Committee for Equality established, starting a year of focus on diversity. The Classics Department in the school already opts for less Eurocentric options where possible in GCSE Ancient History, where Hannibal, the Persian Empire and Alexander the Great's expedition are all featured, and the diversity of the school population is routinely represented in our Key Stage Four and Five classrooms. However, the majority of our students will not stay with us beyond Key Stage Three, where Classical Studies is compulsory in Year Seven, and Latin in Years Eight and

DOI: 10.4324/9781003181958-5

Student perceptions of BAME people in the Roman world 57

Nine. It is therefore pressing, for the sake of those who will stop at that point, as much as for those who are considering continuing their studies and whose decision might depend to some degree on how inclusive we make our teaching, that we foreground representation at the earliest opportunity.

The chance to research this topic arose as we began the process of changing our Key Stage Three teaching materials to the new reading-based course, *Suburani* (Hands Up Education 2020). Our Year Eight students started with *Suburani* at the beginning of the academic year 2020–2021, and continued with it into Year Nine, while the year above continued with our former scheme of work using *Cambridge Latin Course Book 1* (Cambridge School Classics Project 2001), the fourth edition of a reading scheme first published in 1970. This group had also used *Imperium* (Morgan 2013), a more grammatical textbook, during Year Eight, but this is no longer used at the school.

Although the *Cambridge Latin Course* (CLC) has been popular in the UK and US for five decades, it has been criticised both for its lack of representation of women (Sawyer 2016; Amos 2020) and of ethnic minorities (Bracey 2017). It is important to note at this point that the edition to which I will refer throughout is the fourth, in its British version, as this is widely used in UK schools (both in printed copies and the online web book). The authors, the Cambridge School Classics Project (CSCP), implicitly acknowledge this criticism in their Black Lives Matter Statement with the promise that:

> The new UK/International 5th, and all future editions, will better represent people of colour and promote critical engagement with matters such as imperialism, slavery and cultural subjugation.

Further advice for teachers has been provided by CSCP on how to engage with these issues, both in the form of a revised online teachers' guide and blog posts (all nine of which, at the time of writing, either feature BAME classicists or directly address the issue of representation, decolonising the curriculum, and Critical Race Theory). However, active engagement is required on the part of the teacher to seek this advice out and implement it. The legacy fourth edition, and all accompanying resources as presented to students, represent all but one named character in the first book (Syphax, the slave-dealer) as white European. Moreover, although the online fourth edition book has tinted illustrations with a variety of skin tones used for background figures, all characters in the printed copies are represented by black and white line drawings, decreasing the potential visibility of people from non-White ethnic minorities.

Although Hands Up Education does not have a Black Lives Matter Statement per se, the course creators claim (Delaney et al. 2021, 64–65) that they planned for students to 'see the full diversity of the Roman world'. They comment on 'the need for new materials for teachers of Latin to better represent diversity' and acknowledge that,

> ... isotopic analyses of teeth and bones have brought to light a much more ethnically diverse Roman population than has traditionally been portrayed, in both the city of Rome and the Empire.

Miriam Patrick has completed a comprehensive review of the illustrations in *Suburani* (Patrick 2021), but two individuals are worthy of particular mention: Gisco, first appearing in Chapter Two, is identified as Numidian, from North Africa (although this is not explicitly stated in student resources as this stage), and Julia, a minor character appearing solely in Chapter Three and not shown in group images of recurring characters (provided as a printable file in the teacher's resources section of the *Suburani* website), is represented as Black.

Ethnic diversity in the Roman Empire

Before we attempt to improve representation in our own resources, we must have a clear idea of why diversity is necessary in the Classics classroom and what role textbooks have in the creation of the classroom climate. The reasons for representing the ancient world as diverse fall into two broad groups. The first is our duty to teach our subject accurately and to the best of our knowledge, including the clear evidence that the Roman Empire, not least the city of Rome itself, was a diverse place. The second is our responsibility to our students to choose engaging and appropriate resources that reflect the diversity within our school community and in the world for which we are preparing them beyond school. The second was the main driver for undertaking this research, but it became clear during my reading and in discussions with students that the first was little understood, and it prevented full engagement with the second. I will begin by addressing how we might create inclusive classrooms, and how textbook choice contributes to this aim.

The ethnic diversity of the Roman Empire during the imperial period is well established, although how this population might have defined their own ethnicities is a far more complex question. Ancestral DNA analysis (Antonio et al. 2019) of 48 imperial-era individuals demonstrated an 'ancestry shift towards the Eastern Mediterranean and with very few individuals of primarily western European ancestry'. Nor was Rome the only area impacted by this, as Olusoga (2017, 32) comments regarding the Black presence in York:

> The mobility that was a feature of the late Roman Empire may well have meant that parts of 3rd-century Eboracum may well have been more ethnically and racially diverse than parts of York today in the 21st century.

BAME people were not restricted to the lower ranks of society, despite the slave trade and deployment of military recruits from colonised areas to elsewhere in the Empire, such as the unit of Aurelian Moors stationed at Aballava on Hadrian's Wall (Olusoga 2017). He also cites the example of the Ivory Bangle Lady from York, whose grave goods and expensive burial testify to a high status and regard within her community. Thus, the Roman citizen body was described by Beard (2016, 330) as 'the most ethnically diverse there ever was before the modern world'.

There is, nevertheless, a persistent tendency among the anglophone public to underestimate this ethnic diversity of the Greek and Roman world, a trend stoked by the appropriation of Classics by the alt-right. As Donna Zuckerberg argued in her call to arms, *Not All Dead White Men* (2018):

> Anybody who has an interest in the Classics or social justice should care about the trend of using the literature and history of ancient Greece and Rome to promote patriarchal and white supremacist ideology. This movement has the potential to reshape what ancient Greece and Rome mean in the 21st century, while simultaneously promoting dangerous and discriminatory views about gender and race.

An example of this framing of the classical past as an artificially white reality was seen in the backlash that followed two BBC productions: *Roman Britain* (2014) and *Troy: Fall of a City* (2018). The former, a six-minute schools' video depicting a Black Roman officer in Britain loosely based on the career of the real-life Quintus Lollius Urbicus, a second-century CE governor of Britain, of North African descent, resulted in several days of abusive tweets directed towards Mary Beard for having described this as 'pretty accurate' (Beard 2017 tweet). The casting of several Black actors as both heroes and deities in *Troy: Fall of a City* once again brought strong criticism for 'Blackwashing' on both Twitter and YouTube, this time countered by Tim Whitmarsh (Regius Professor of Greek at the University of Cambridge) who highlighted that 'any attempt to answer the question of what Ancient Greeks looked like has to be led by genetic research, not by assumptions' (Whitmarsh 2018). In this context, we should be alert to the possibility that depictions of BAME individuals in our teaching materials, especially those in high-status positions, might be perceived by some learners as unrealistic unless supported by clear evidence from biological, historical and archaeological sources (Snowden 1997).

Reviewing positionality

Before I could evaluate the importance of inclusive materials to my students, I took the time to begin evaluating my own privilege and the way in which my own background as a white British person had influenced my approach to the subject. The following two statements on Peggy McIntosh's autobiographical list of her own experiences of privilege in *Unpacking the Invisible Knapsack* (McIntosh 1989) resonated particularly with me and were relevant to the non-inclusive teaching of history:

> 6. When I am told about our national heritage or about 'civilization,' I am shown that people of my color made it what it is.
>
> 7. I can be sure that my children will be given curricular materials that testify to the existence of their race.

These both fall into her category of 'unearned entitlement' which should, in a just world, be extended to all: no student should feel that people with whom they identify are excluded from the corpus of what is deemed worthy of study, and especially not of those parts that are celebrated with loaded terms such as 'Classics'. Ambrose et al. (2010) created a classification of classroom climates for college classes, which can be applied to Classics teaching at school level to evaluate the level of marginalisation or inclusion, and the mechanisms (actively teacher-led or passively permitted) by which this operates. The explicitly marginalising class is one in which material is drawn exclusively from the white, elite, male perspective. The implicitly marginalising class excludes more subtly (for instance, by treating other perspectives as digressions which should be avoided). The implicitly centralising class accepts such perspectives, but leaves the onus on the students, and the explicitly centralising plans and allows time for these perspectives. Gellar-Goad's (2015) article applying Ambrose's work to Ancient Greek and Latin teaching in the American college context raises a particular challenge for our discipline:

> A centralizing climate requires extra care to achieve when teaching a language and literature like Latin or Greek whose survival has by and large depended on a canonization process controlled by elite men.

Although this might initially seem to apply only to older age groups accessing literature as part of assessed courses with prescribed original texts, it can be seen as trickling through into the composition of stories adapted for reading even at earlier ages, such as the apparent influence of Roman comedy on the 'Happy Slave' motif observed by Dugan (2019) in the *Cambridge Latin Course* inter alia. She singles out textbook choice or, failing that, contextualisation of problematic representations within the textbook, as ways of avoiding marginalising climates. American teacher John Bracey (2017) also included poor choice of resources as a contributing factor in his article 'Why Students of Color Don't Take Latin':

> It is easy for even the most well-intentioned Latin teacher to inadvertently alienate students of color—for example, by centering a course around a textbook that speaks glowingly about how much Roman occupation improved the lives of their subjects and also contains no images of people of color.

Thus, the choice of coursebook is a key element in constructing an atmosphere that is inclusive of all. There are good reasons for arguing that representation in a textbook is more important even than representation in literary and historical sources, which are more likely to be contextualised and questioned by the teacher and class. Edwards (2008, 39), writing as a history teacher, observes that the ubiquitous textbook is surprisingly unexamined by teachers:

> … we continue to treat textbooks as if they were sources of 'safe' knowledge and we put aside our customary need for a critical stance. We hand out to our class sets as if they were immaculately conceived and somehow miss the point that they are constructed too and as such are partial.

Sleeter and Grant (1991) also argue that the ways in which textbooks create and project symbolic representations of society are hidden and not explicit to the viewer:

> ... symbolic representations in the curriculum represent socially constructed relations as natural; subjective interpretations of reality and value judgements are presented as fact.

This is particularly acute in the case of the school-age learner, who, when compared with the scholar and teacher, is less likely to access resources that show differing perspectives. The content of the textbook is likely to be a highly partial view from the perspective of the more privileged:

> Usually controlled and produced by dominant groups, materials and other media confirm the status of those groups whose culture and accomplishments are deemed important enough to write about.

This is broadly confirmed by Sleeter and Grant's analysis of 47 American textbooks for first to eighth grades (Years Two to Nine) published between 1980 and 1988. Although illustrations and stories featured a variety of ethnic groups, women and people with disabilities, common flaws included gender stereotyping and including the visible markers of difference (such as skin tone) without authentically reflecting the lived experiences of different groups (such as cultural differences or the economic realities of working-class life). Minorities were frequently seen in passive roles (such as those with disabilities merely sitting in illustrations, without being engaged in the action, or the infrequency with which Asian American, Hispanic and Indigenous Americans were depicted as solving their own challenges). Moreover, collective identities and the roles of dominant groups in perpetrating racism were glossed over.

Sawyer says, in 'Latin for all Identities' (2016, 35–36), that:

> Simply adding a minority character to a textbook storyline, for example, is not a successful means of positive representation and inclusion. You may have heard the phrase 'diversity is counting people; inclusion is when people count.' Diversity is the very least we can do.

She uses the *Cambridge Latin Course* (UK Fourth Edition) as her main example of an unrepresentative course, referring to the inactivity of the female characters, and the failure of *Book 2* to fairly replicate in its choice of characters the diversity that it discusses in Roman Alexandria. She places the burden of redressing the balance with more diverse images from teachers' own examples and using the faults in the textbook as 'teachable moments'.

I also looked for guidelines on decolonising the curricula of comparable disciplines, particularly those with historic links to imperialism. Those produced by the School of Oriental and African Studies, although intended for tertiary education, are applicable also to secondary. 'Decolonising SOAS: Learning and Teaching Toolkit for Module Conveners' (May 2018) poses the following applicable questions:

> Who is represented as an 'Other' in my teaching and how?
>
> Is this potentially problematic and for whom?

To apply this to a story-based course, we need to ask ourselves whether there are characters depicted as outside the main group. The sole BAME character in the *Cambridge Latin Course Book 1* (UK Fourth Edition) is potentially such a character: Syphax the slave-dealer, whose portrayal is limited to two main aspects: his ethnicity (Syrian) and his trade.

Research methodology

As decolonisation of our school's curriculum is an ongoing process, and the school year (2020–2021) was already constrained by lockdown teaching, it was necessary to focus on one narrow element: the presentation of BAME individuals in Roman society. The term BAME was kept throughout despite the problematic way in which it implies that the experience of all non-white people is parallel, owing to the difficulty of mapping more precise modern ethnic groups onto the Roman population and, in particular, to the depictions in Latin textbooks. Participation in the process was voluntary and opportunities were provided to self-identify with more specific ethnicities.

Quantifiable data was initially collected via a Google Form Questionnaire sent to all of my classes and some of my colleagues' classes during the second half of the spring term. This was kept brief to encourage high rates of participation and featured three Likert scale questions: how many BAME people the student thought there were in Roman society, how many there were in their book and how positively or negatively they were presented. To check the reliability of their answers, they were also asked if they could name any of the BAME characters in the book. All names that could be recognised were included regardless of variant spellings ('Lulia' instead of 'Iulia', for example): only names that could not be securely identified were excluded from results. To mitigate the impact of remote teaching on their recall, I used a pair of Kahoot quizzes the week prior to the survey, made as closely parallel as possible, asking students to match the names to the 11 characters displayed. Each of the responses on the Likert scales was assigned a number (for instance, 1 for 'very positively' to 5 for 'very negatively'), so that an average score could be found for each year-group's answers to each question. This enabled scores for Years Eight and Nine to be compared. In the course of one year, it was not possible to control for other differences between the year-groups (such as maturity): repeating the questionnaires the following year would therefore be desirable.

The second phase of the data collection used focus groups to deepen the understanding of the impact on students of how the textbooks presented people from BAME backgrounds. A question was included in the survey asking whether students would be willing to participate in this, and those who replied 'yes' or 'maybe' were contacted via email with further details. Initially, these were scheduled for lunchtimes on return to school, late in the spring term. As turnout was too low to be viable, these were rescheduled with the assistance of form tutors for extended registrations in May. The sessions were necessarily short, and question prompts focused on whether the depictions were felt to be realistic, whether this mattered to the students, and what improvements, if any, could be made. As the focus groups (consisting of 12 students in Year Nine and 10 in Year Eight) were self-selecting, it was not possible to balance the representation of ethnic groups: this resulted in an over-representation of students who identified as Asian and no representation of Black students.

Findings: survey

A total of 106 Year Eight students (aged 12–13) and 79 Year Nine students (aged 13–14) replied to the survey. The average Year Eight was aware of one BAME person in their coursebook, whereas the average for the Year Nine students was between one and none. This was even closer to 'none' among Year Nine students who identified themselves as BAME, although the answers did not differ for Year Eight. Some 61 per cent of Year Nine students, rising to 81 per cent of Year Nine BAME students, were not aware of any BAME characters in their book. The comparable results for Year Eight were less than half this: 30 per cent and 29 per cent (Table 4.1).

This was supported by their ability to name BAME characters: 27 Year Nine students identified Julia and 7 named Gisco, but only 3 Year Nine students could name Syphax. This was partially reflective

Student perceptions of BAME people in the Roman world 65

Table 4.1 Pupil responses to the first survey question: Are there any BAME characters in your Latin course book? This question refers to your Suburani textbook/Activebook if you are in Year Eight, and the Cambridge Latin Course Book 1/web book if you are in Year Nine

Year	0: No response	1: Yes, more than one	2: Yes, one	3: None	Total
8	1%	36%	33%	30%	100%
9	3%	18%	18%	62%	100%

of a greater willingness to venture a name on the part of the younger group (52 answers, compared with only 5 from the older year). There was a surprisingly large number of votes for the (blonde) Quartilla, perhaps reflecting some confusion between the large number of female characters in the *Suburani* course (Table 4.2).

This difference appears to be reflected in the average students' estimations of BAME people as a proportion of Roman society. Both years thought this was a minority, but Year Nine believed it was closer to a small minority than Year Eight. The results for BAME students mirrored those of the sample as a whole. Similarly to the previous question, the percentage of Year Eight students who believed that there were no BAME people in the Roman world (six per cent) was under half the percentage of Year Nine who held this belief (14 per cent), and considerably less than the 26 per cent of Year Nine BAME students who did (Table 4.3).

Findings: focus groups

In the Year Nine focus group, some students argued that the limited representation of BAME people was appropriate for the setting:

> I think that it doesn't show many BAME people in the book but that's accurate.
>
> (Year Nine student F)

Table 4.2 Pupil responses to the second survey question: How many Black, Asian or minority ethnic (BAME) people do you think there were in Roman society?

Year	1: A majority	2: About half	3: A minority	4: A small minority	5: None	Total
8	5%	16%	32%	42%	6%	100%
9	1%	8%	30%	47%	14%	100%

Table 4.3 Pupil responses to the third survey question: If you answered yes, how do you think BAME characters are portrayed in the book?

Year	0: No response	1: Very positively	2: Positively	3: Neither positively nor negatively	4: Negatively	5: Very negatively	Total
8	22%	5%	15%	53%	5%	1%	100%
9	48%	0%	5%	24%	18%	5%	100%

> I don't think there'd be many people from a different ... different ethnicities coming to like Rome or like Greece into those sort of areas so representation of these people in these places as shown in the textbook so it is quite accurate I think, what is shown in the textbook.
>
> (Year Nine student H)

Others argued that it should have been higher:

> ... there must have been some BAME people in like the Greek and Roman times, so, I just feel like I can't see any of it really.
>
> (Year Nine student M)

They sometimes drew on background knowledge of the Roman Empire or recalled topics covered in Year Seven Classical Studies to justify this, with varying degrees of accuracy:

> ... if this is set around the time of Mount Vesuvius destroying Pompeii it would be coming close to the time Rome would be at its height and in that case we would be seeing Britons, Anglos, Gauls ... we would be seeing a lot more of ethnic groups from the span of the empire which obviously shows that there isn't enough representation for them.
>
> (Year Nine student K)

> I think it may actually not show a fair representation, as when you think about it there many multi-ethnic people in the Roman world from Greeks to Romans to people from France and it doesn't really show people from France and other cultures who came into the Roman Empire, it mainly focuses more on Greeks and Romans.
>
> (Year Nine student G)

> I think that in the Romans obviously they had quite a big empire and also there were Persians there.
>
> (Year Nine student J)

One notable aspect of this discussion was the apparent lack of certainty regarding geographic origins of people expected to be found in the Roman Empire: only one mention was made of Africa, but several to France, and some to Persia.

Students in the Year Eight focus group, in contrast, were aware of the representation of diversity and regarded this as a positive from the point of view of inclusion:

> ... if they're different ethnicities it helps you relate more to the people.
> (Year Eight student D)

> ... there's a lot of minority ethnic groups popping up, which is good.
> (Year Eight student B)

Two students, however, regarded this as an inaccuracy:

> I feel like to improve the book they should of course keep the ethnic minority groups in because that really helps balance and helps relate to the people who read the book but there should be some sort of disclaimer somewhere which says that it's not exactly how Roman times would have been.
> (Year Eight student C)

This was echoed in the Year Nine group by an apparent assumption that Roman and BAME identities were mutually exclusive:

> ... it's a Roman textbook about Latin, so you probably expect it to be about Romans, which is probably why it's focusing on Romans rather than BAME.
> (Year Nine student F)

Furthermore, some members of both groups expressed the opinion that inclusion was not important to the core function of Latin resources and therefore not particularly important to them:

> ... you're not really learning about races, you're learning about Latin so, to me, I don't mind what kind of ethnicities I see in the book.
> (Year Eight student B)

> I don't really think that it matters whether we see different people of different ethnicities, coming to be presented in the book because that's not the purpose of the book the purpose of the

book is to explain and show how Romans lived at that time and also to teach the Latin, the language of Latin.

(Year Nine student H)

Given the prevalence of the assumption that Roman people were *ipso facto* unlikely to be BAME, it was unsurprising that when asked how teachers could improve representation, they suggested stretching the geographical extent of the course:

... what teachers more can do is that they can do maybe one or two lessons on showing different parts of the empire instead of just staying on the Italian peninsula.

(Year Nine student K)

Indeed, both courses do use this approach, but students had not at this point read far enough to encounter it. One student suggested a focus on trading connections:

... when you're in the trading part of the textbook we could talk about French goods or like English goods from other places.

(Year Nine student G)

Neither of these, however, would in themselves show BAME characters in Roman Italy.

A second set of suggestions centred around showing culture as well as colour. One student suggested that the names of characters could be used to show differing origins:

I don't think it represents the, I guess, names that might be given to babies of like Asia or like Eurasia so that may be a factor that could be used to see how BAME people are represented in the book.

(Year Nine student H)

Another suggested religious identities could be explored:

... they could talk about what the religions of the ethnicities were.

(Year Eight student E)

Although these suggestions are more complex than the students are likely to have realised, owing to the name changes imposed by slave owners, the importance of the *tria nomina* for an individual acquiring citizenship and the syncretising tendencies of Roman religion, both of these requests show an enthusiasm for exploring the ways in which ethnic minorities expressed their own identities.

Conclusions

A textbook which represents the diversity of the Roman world in an accurate and accessible way is a useful tool for teaching Latin, and it makes a difference to some students' assumptions about the ancient world. However, an increase in the visibility of BAME people in pictures and stories is not in itself sufficient. BAME characters should have an impact on the plot to have an impact on student perceptions. The onus is therefore still on the Classics teacher to draw links between the plot and the evidence available for ethnic minorities within the Roman Empire. Where possible, this should explore these people's experiences, actions and culture, and their interactions with other Romans. For many, this is likely to be an aspect of their subject that was not explicitly discussed in their own initial teacher training or degree, and there is a need for professional development opportunities, perhaps provided by the national charitable bodies for the promotion of Classical Studies.

At a departmental level, this should be incorporated explicitly into the curriculum and taken into account when choosing resources, both the main coursebook (where funding permits a change) and supplementary materials (such as displays, video clips, images on slide shows and worksheets). There is also work for publishers to do, particularly in using the background sections of a book, to clarify the historicity of representations of BAME people within the stories. Teachers' notes and the resource sections of supporting websites could be updated with guidance, information and supplementary sources. If we are to expand Classics in a responsible and critically reflective way, we should consider, as a subject community, how we can contribute to the curriculum decolonisation process. This project has shown that, when asked, students have interesting and constructive comments on the learning materials they encounter.

Note

1 'BAME' is a problematic term; it groups together people from diverse ethnicities, implies homogeneity and simplifies the relationship between race and ethnicity. It has been used in this chapter because it was used in school policy during the conduct of this research.

Reference List

Ambrose, S. A., M. W. Bridges, M. DiPietro, M. C. Lovett and M. K. Norman. 2010. "Why Do Student Development and Course Climate Matter for Student Learning?". In *How Learning Works: Seven Research-Based Principles for Smart Teaching*, 153–187. New York City: Wiley.

Amos, E. 2020. "A case study investigation of student perceptions of women as seen in the Cambridge Latin Course in a selective girls' grammar school". *Journal of Classics Teaching* 21 (42): 5–13.

Antonio, M. L. et al. 2019. "Ancient Rome: A genetic crossroads of Europe and the Mediterranean". *Science* 366 (6466): 708–714.

Beard, M. 2016. *SPQR: A History of Ancient Rome*. London: Profile.

Beard, M. (@wmarybeard). 2017. "This is indeed pretty accurate, there's plenty of firm evidence for ethnic diversity in Roman Britain". *Twitter*, 25 July. Accessed 30 May 2021. https://twitter.com/wmarybeard/status/889925415032299520?lang=en.

Bracey, J. 2017. "Why Students of Colour Don't take Classics". *Eidolon*. Accessed 31 May 2021. https://eidolon.pub/why-students-of-color-dont-take-latin-4ddee3144934.

Cambridge School Classics Project. 2001. *Cambridge Latin Course Book 1*. UK Fourth Edition Cambridge: Cambridge University Press.

Cambridge School Classics Project. 2020. "Black Lives Matter Statement". Accessed 22 June 2021. https://www.cambridgescp.com/black-lives-matter-statement-cscp.

Council of University Classics Departments. 2020. "Equality and Diversity in Classics Report". Accessed 13 January 2022. https://cucd.blogs.sas.ac.uk/files/2020/11/CUCD-Equality-and-Diversity-Report-2020.pdf.

Decolonising SOAS Working Group. 2018. "Decolonising SOAS Learning and Teaching Toolkit for Programme and Module Convenors May 2018". Accessed 22 June 2021. https://blogs.soas.ac.uk/decolonisingsoas/files/2018/10/Decolonising-SOAS-Learning-and-Teaching-Toolkit-AB.pdf.

Delaney, C., H. Smith, L. Tims, T. Smith and W. Griffiths. 2021. "Keeping the ancient world relevant for modern students with *Suburani*". *Journal of Classics Teaching* 22 (43): 64–67.

Dugan, K. P. 2019. "The 'Happy Slave' Narrative and Classics Pedagogy: A Verbal and Visual Analysis of Beginning Greek and Latin Textbooks". *New England Classical Journal* 46 (1): 62–87.

Edwards, C. 2008. "The How of History: Using Old and New Textbooks in the Classroom to Develop Disciplinary Knowledge". *Teaching History* 130: 39–45.

Gellar-Goad, T. 2015. "How learning works in the Greek and Latin classroom, Part 7". Accessed 23 June 2021. https://classicalstudies.org/blogs/ted-gellar-goad/how-learning-works-greek-and-latin-classroom-part-7.

Hands Up Education. 2020. *Suburani*. Haverhill: Hands Up Education.

Joseph-Salisbury, R. 2020. *Race and Racism in English Secondary Schools*. London: Runnymede. Accessed 24 June 2021. https://www.runnymedetrust.org/uploads/publications/pdfs/Runnymede%20Secondary%20Schools%20report%20FINAL.pdf.

Ling, T. 2018. "No, the BBC is not "Blackwashing" Troy: Fall of a City". Accessed 23 June 2021. https://www.radiotimes.com/tv/drama/troy-fall-of-a-city-blackwashing-casting-black-actors-greek-myth/.

McIntosh, P. 1989. "Unpacking the Invisible Knapsack". Accessed 24 June 2021. https://nationalseedproject.org/Key-SEED-Texts/white-privilege-unpacking-the-invisible-knapsack.

Morgan, J. 2013. "Imperium Latin Course". Published online. Accessed 24 June 2021. http://www.imperiumlatin.com/

Olusoga, D. 2017. *Black and British: A Forgotten History*. London: Pan Macmillan.

Patrick, M. 2021. "Suburani: Part 1". *Mater Monstrorum Blog*, 24 March. Accessed 28 February 2022. https://www.matermonstrorum.com/social-justice/suburani-par-1.

Sawyer, B. 2016. "Latin for all identities". *The Journal of Classics Teaching* 17 (33): 35–39. Accessed 31 May 2021. https://www.cambridge.org/core/journals/journal-of-classics-teaching/article/latin-for-all-identities/ABA26AD3FA0167FA2AEB2AA7C35B3202.

Sleeter, C. E. and C. A. Grant. 1991. "Race, Class, Gender and Disability in Current Textbooks". In *The Politics of the Textbook*, edited by M. Apple and L. K. Christian, 78–110. New York: Routledge.

Snowden, F. M. 1997. "Misconceptions about African Blacks in the Ancient Mediterranean World: Specialists and Afrocentrists". *Arion: A Journal of Humanities and the Classics* 4 (3): 28–50.

Warwick Classics Network. 2022. "Diversity/BAME Teaching Resources". Accessed 13 January 2022. https://warwick.ac.uk/fac/arts/classics/warwickclassicsnetwork/stoa/bame/.

Whitmarsh, T. 2018. "Black Achilles". *Aeon*, 9 May. Accessed 23 June 2021. https://aeon.co/essays/when-homer-envisioned-achilles-did-he-see-a-black-man.

Zuckerberg, D. 2018. *Not All Dead White Men: Classics and Misogyny in the Digital Age*. Cambridge: Harvard University Press.

5 Promoting inclusivity through teaching Ancient History

Anna McOmish

Introduction

To understand the value and significance of the study of the Ancient Middle East in the Key Stage Three (KS3) curriculum at Aldridge School, one must first understand the socio-economic characteristics of the school's catchment area. If one were to search for 'Aldridge School' and assess the socio-economic characteristics of the area, they would find a predominantly white and relatively affluent population. Aldridge Central and South, the immediate area around the school, is 92 per cent White British, eight per cent minority ethnic, and only 40 households (0.7 per cent of the total) in the area have no one in the house speaking English as the main language (Walsall Council 2011). It also has low levels of economic deprivation, with an average Index of Multiple Deprivation (IMD) score[1] of 15.0 (Connolly 2019). However, Aldridge School's catchment area extends into Central and Eastern Walsall, which are within the top ten per cent of the most deprived areas in England. By including postcodes WS1, WS2 and WS4, Aldridge School educates students from areas such as Blakenall, where the average IMD score is 53.6, and St Matthew's, where the average IMD score is 38.2 (Connolly 2019). In comparison to Aldridge Central and South, 77 per cent of Walsall residents are White British, and 23 per cent are minority ethnic, with 15 per cent being Asian minority ethnic (Connolly 2013).

As a result, Aldridge is a diverse school, ethnically, economically and socially. Aldridge educates approximately 1600 pupils, aged 11–18; 12 per cent of pupils have English as an Additional Language (EAL) (the national average in secondary schools in 2019 was 17 per cent); and the number of students claiming their right to free school meals in 2019 was 18 per cent (the national average in secondary schools in 2019 was 14 per cent), but the number of pupils eligible for Free School

DOI: 10.4324/9781003181958-6

Meals at any time during the past six years stands at 34 per cent (Department for Education 2019). The expansion of Ancient History at Aldridge has been largely unaffected by these factors. The History department at Aldridge is staffed by nine teachers. At the time of writing, the department includes one early career teacher, three staff with more than five years of experience, including an OCR examiner, the Head of Humanities, one Pastoral head, two Assistant Heads and a Deputy Head. Students have the option of selecting one of two History GCSEs (ages 14–16), History or Ancient History, and can then choose to study either or both at A-Level (ages 16–18). I believe that it is this combination of the diversity of the student body, the range of subjects available at Key Stage Four and Key Stage Five, together with the ability of a highly experienced staff body to teach two historical subjects at examination level which has facilitated the success of Ancient History at Aldridge.

Ancient History in the Aldridge curriculum

In 2015, the History department at Aldridge was teaching the AQA Classical Civilisation GCSE and A-Level and, although student numbers were small, exam results were strong. Until 2017, low uptake, particularly at GCSE, resulted from a perception that 'Class Civ' was only for more able students. Although this self-selecting process aided strong results and able A-Level groups, it did not encourage the widest range of students to access classical subjects. The decision to switch from teaching Classical Civilisation GCSE/A-Level to teaching Ancient History was made as a result of the 2017 A-Level reforms.[2] Changes to the AQA Classical Civilisation A-Level emphasised classical philosophy, which was not popular among staff. At Aldridge, we had always chosen the 'historical' A-Level units on offer with AQA Classical Civilisation. We therefore decided to change both subject and exam board and began teaching GCSE and A-Level OCR Ancient History from the autumn of 2017.

The Ancient History GCSE was immediately popular. Our first cohort had 60+ students split across two classes, and given our non-selective intake and the socio-economic range of our students discussed above, this cohort was truly mixed in ability. Pupils' target grades ranged from a 2 to a 9 (Grade 9 is the highest available at GCSE). Supporting the first GCSE cohort to examination level presented challenges and highlighted the need for changes to the pre-GCSE curriculum. The biggest issue staff faced was facilitating the understanding of our academically weaker students as they began to study an entirely new period of history. Although students enjoyed the interesting and unusual narratives that Ancient History provides (such as the accession of Darius I to the throne via horse-related trickery), the challenging nature of the GCSE presented difficulties for some. High attaining students worked quickly through the content and were happy to engage with complicated source analysis and detailed chronologies (as shown by 2019 GCSE results where around 33 per cent of the cohort received a 7–9 grade). Whereas students with weaker literacy skills struggled to read extended sources and chronologies (as shown by our 2019 results where seven students across two classes received a U grade).[3]

Thus, for students to enjoy Ancient History AND be academically successful in it, we realised that it was vital to expose them to Ancient History earlier in their education. All students could therefore have more time to become familiar with the chronologies and geographies required at GCSE and they would be developing the skills required for success in the Ancient History course.

Including Ancient History in the KS3 curriculum

In the summer term of 2019 (prior to the first set of GCSE results), the KS3 curriculum was adapted to include an Ancient History topic in each KS3 year group (Year Seven to Year Nine), lasting one half term each (approximately six to eight weeks) (Table 5.1).

Including an Ancient History topic in each year broke from the chronology of that year's study, and, as a department, we decided that we would explicitly communicate this to our students. We warned them of the chronological break in the lead up to the new term, explained the purpose of doing so – supporting GCSE learning and cementing a deeper understanding of historical themes in the KS3 curriculum – and referenced connecting themes throughout the teaching of the topics.

Table 5.1 The KS3 History curriculum at Aldridge School with changes from summer 2019 in bold

Year Seven	Year Eight	Year Nine
Norman Conquest	English Civil War	**Ancient Middle East**
Medieval Monarchs	Industrial Revolution	Origins of WWI
Medieval Life	Atlantic Slave Trade	WWI/Interwar years
Wars of the Roses	British Empire	WWII
Tudor Life	Civil Rights Movement	Nazi Germany
Ancient Greece	**Ancient Rome**	The Cold War

Why make these changes?

Two key factors helped us make this decision. Firstly, we wanted students to have a better understanding of the content and skills of Ancient History in preparation for success at GCSE. As mentioned previously, our first GCSE cohort produced mixed results, and we had at least six students for whom it was not the right GCSE choice, but they chose it because it was 'new' and 'unknown'. It was also clear that to support the building of knowledge and understanding at GCSE, we had to be doing more to support understanding and foundational knowledge leading up to Year Ten (when we start the GCSE course). By including Ancient History in our KS3 curriculum, we were creating a spiral curriculum that would allow students to develop the foundational schemata necessary to be able to absorb and understand more complicated history at Key Stage Four and beyond.

Bruner's spiral curriculum model was originally designed for the teaching of sciences and posits that concepts being taught to a student should be introduced repeatedly across the learning timeframe, starting with basic versions of the concept building towards advanced concepts as time/learning develops (Bruner 1960). Topics, concepts and ideas should be revisited at increasing levels of complexity as the spiral (students' time in education) loops higher and higher (Ireland and Mouthaan 2020). By including Ancient History relating to fifth-century Greece, Rome 753 BCE to CE 476, and the Ancient Middle East 3000–479 BCE in our KS3 curriculum, it ensured that the content students needed to know for Ancient History GCSE (and A-Level) was being introduced in more simplistic forms from which students could generalise the information for reuse later in their studies (Bruner 1960) (Figure 5.1).

The benefit of including Ancient History in the KS3 curriculum was clear. The GCSE content was no longer completely novel to our Year Ten students, and students from the 2020/2021 cohort have consistently recalled KS3 learning in their GCSE lessons when studying the Persian Empire unit. For example, because pupils study the significance of Babylon in Year Nine, in Year Ten they can better understand and analyse why it was so important that Cyrus the Great conquered the same city in 539 BCE.

Secondly, we wanted to create a diverse curriculum, in the sense of autonomous and positive representation of people from BAME backgrounds.[4] Although significant strides have been made with the inclusion of Black history in curricula across the country, by the summer of 2019, we were becoming increasingly concerned that the same was

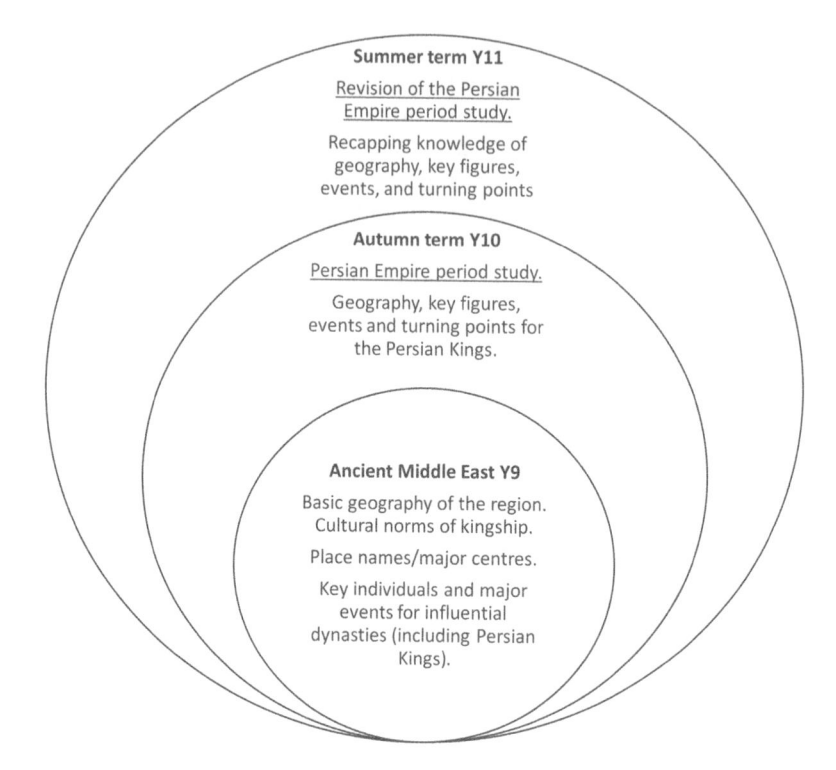

Summer term Y11
Revision of the Persian Empire period study.
Recapping knowledge of geography, key figures, events, and turning points

Autumn term Y10
Persian Empire period study.
Geography, key figures, events and turning points for the Persian Kings.

Ancient Middle East Y9
Basic geography of the region.
Cultural norms of kingship.
Place names/major centres.
Key individuals and major events for influential dynasties (including Persian Kings).

Figure 5.1 This figure illustrates how including study of the Ancient Middle East in the KS3 curriculum supported students' learning in their subsequent GCSE topic on the Persian Empire, creating a spiral curriculum that established beneficial schemata.

not the case for histories relating to Islamic peoples or modern geographical regions with large Muslim populations. Data from the academic year 2020/2021 showed that 19 per cent of the Aldridge student body identified as Asian Pakistani, the largest of our BAME groups. Additionally, within my own research, 96 per cent of students who identified as Asian Pakistani also identified as Muslim (McOmish 2021), meaning that it was reasonable to assume that the majority of the 19 per cent of Asian Pakistani students also identified as Muslim. Thus, histories relating to Islamic peoples or geographical regions with some historical relevance to modern day Islamic students should be better represented in our curriculum.

By Summer 2019, we were concerned that our KS3 curriculum bordered on what Matthew Williamson has referred to as an 'absent curriculum' (Wilkinson 2014a). When Asian Islamic history or geographical areas synonymous with Islamic populations were being studied, it was in relation to their interaction with Europe and Europeans. Wilkinson's study assessing the impact of a lack of Islamic and Asian history in the curriculum on Muslim students in secondary schools posited that for a topic to not be considered by policymakers, not considered by SLT and teachers, and then not be discussed in the classroom is to send the message that the topic is not important and therefore the types of people it includes are not relevant in the study of history. In doing so, one creates a curriculum that is defined by its absence, and Wilkinson argued that the distinct lack of Muslim history in the curriculum, or Muslim history that shows positive autonomy, disengages Muslim boys (Wilkinson 2014b).

Similarly, when working with a boys' comprehensive in London, Whitburn and Yemoh challenged the inclusion of 'standard' Black history units, such as 'Civil Rights', and instead produced a unique GCSE unit on the challenges of establishing a multicultural Britain in the post-war era. Like Wilkinson, they found that ethnic minority students responded more positively to their learning when the curriculum content expanded to include multiple historical narratives, especially those which highlighted autonomous historical achievements of ethnic minorities present within the school cohort (Whitburn and Yemoh 2012). We therefore wanted to provide areas of study where the history was independent of European involvement and was a positive representation of that area for the sake of the achievements of its people.

These two key factors very purposefully drove us towards the inclusion of Ancient History in our KS3 curriculum, and it is our study of the Ancient Middle East 3000–479 BCE where this has come to fruition most effectively.

The Ancient Middle East 3000–479 BCE

The chronological range for this Year Nine unit was large as we aimed for students to develop a clear understanding of the geography of the area and the timeline of events that led up to and included the Persian Empire depth study in the Ancient History GCSE (Table 5.2).

The topic included 12 lessons under two enquiry questions (EQs).

Enquiry question 1 – How far was this the 'Cradle of Civilisation'?

Taking inspiration from Stephen Bourke's *The Middle East: The Cradle of Civilization Revealed*, which was used in planning for this

Table 5.2 Ancient Middle East 3000–479 BCE: enquiry questions and lesson order

The Ancient Middle East 3000–479 BCE	*Enquiry question*	*Lesson title*
	Lessons 1–4: how far was this the 'Cradle of Civilisation'?	The city of Ur The new Hittite Kingdom The Battle of Qadesh The Sea Peoples (Bronze Age Collapse) CHANGE OF ENQUIRY QUESTION
	Lessons 5–12: which was the most successful dynasty of the Ancient Middle East?	Assyria: Ashurnasirpal II Assyria: Tiglath-Pileser II Assyria: Ashurbanipal Assyria to Babylon Babylon: Nebuchadnezzar Persia: Cyrus the Great Persia: Cambyses Persia: Darius

unit, the first EQ introduced students to evidence that has helped create the idea of the area being the 'cradle of civilisation' (Bourke 2008). This EQ surveyed major events up until the Bronze Age collapse around 1200 BCE, which would allow students to assess the validity of this idea. 'The City of Ur' introduced students to the significance of the fertile crescent, the developments in science, maths, farming and engineering that took place in the area, as well as the organisation and achievements of the city of Ur. All of these helped students critically evaluate the idea of the Ancient Middle East as the 'Cradle of Civilisation'.

Subsequent lessons gave an overview of the kings of the new Hittite dynasty, focusing on the accession and achievements of each king. Students focused on comparative work between the kings and built upon the idea that the area was creating strongly led and 'civilised' kingdoms. The final lessons within the EQ investigated the Bronze Age collapse of 1200 BCE. Initially focusing on 'The Sea Peoples', the first lesson studied the origins and consequences of the Bronze Age collapse, analysing ancient sources such as the letter from Ugarit and the Egyptian relief of the battle of the Delta to understand contemporary ideas about the causes of the collapse. The second lesson used modern interpretations to understand recent hypotheses behind the collapse, leading students to assess how far the area was 'the Cradle of Civilisation' if this event could have such devastating consequences for the area.

Enquiry question 2 – Which was the most successful dynasty of the Ancient Middle East?

The second EQ analysed the characteristics and achievements of some of the most significant dynasties of the Ancient Middle East, ending with a study of the first three Achaemenid kings which is a compulsory element of the Ancient History GCSE. Considering the Neo-Assyrians, the Babylonians and the Achaemenids, this EQ enabled students to develop skills of analysis and evaluation by comparing dynasties under their own definition of 'success', and to draw thematic comparisons to other areas of the KS3 curriculum. Themes such as nation-building, empire, kingship and warfare were present in the unit and had also been discussed at various points throughout Year Seven and Year Eight.

The first lessons studied the Neo-Assyrian kings (hereafter referred to as 'the Assyrians') and were popular with our students. These lessons assessed the origins of the Assyrians, how far Ashurnasirpal II was a pragmatist or a megalomaniac, the expansion under Tiglath-Pileser II, the importance of his wife Queen Yaba, and ended with studying Ashurbanipal and his approach to education and state-building. These lessons were rich in material culture and evaluated the successes of the Assyrians as well as various factors that led to the fall of Assyria and the rise of Babylon/King Nabopolassar. Lessons then focused specifically on the actions of Nebuchadnezzar II in expanding Babylonian territory and improving Babylon. The final lessons of the unit looked at three out of four of the Achaemenid kings – Cyrus the Great, Cambyses II and Darius I. In these lessons, students consistently used ancient sources such as Herodotus, the Cyrus Cylinder and the Bisitun Inscription to allow students first-hand access to the history.

Assessment

This unit's assessment centred on an essay-style question where students were asked to use their own knowledge and ancient sources to respond to the question: '"Ashurnasirpal was the most successful of the Ancient Middle Eastern Kings". How far do you agree with this statement?' It was a response to this assessment question that sparked my interest in researching student perceptions of this unit, and particularly the responses of Muslim students. An Asian male Muslim student in my class, whom I had taught since Year Eight and who had shown average engagement until Year Nine, completed this assessment and handed to me a four-page, informed and compellingly argued response as to why Ashurbanipal was the most successful of the Ancient Middle Eastern kings. It remains to this day one of the most enjoyable assessments I have ever read.

The impact

Given the dual aims of including this Ancient Middle East topic in the curriculum, I was interested in the responses of the students and keen to engage in meaningful research as to its impact on Muslim students. As a result of Wilkinson's research, and my own perceptions of the gaps in our KS3 curriculum, my research question looked to understand how Muslim students were impacted by being taught a KS3 unit on the Ancient Middle East. Positive patterns emerged from my data in relation to the engagement, connection and perceived success of Muslim students – that is to say, their academic attainment, knowledge retention, intellectual curiosity and subject engagement – as well as the interest levels of students of other ethnic/religious backgrounds. The research[5] was conducted using a mixed method approach of quantitative and qualitative methods, and concerned data and feedback from the 2020/2021 Year Nine cohort. Data from 108 quantitative questionnaires from four Year Nine classes was combined with the qualitative output from eight semi-structured interviews, to inform the overall findings on the impact of teaching the Ancient Middle East at KS3.

Research findings

In my analysis, I concluded that four important findings could be confirmed from this data, all of which make clear the benefits of including Ancient History in the KS3 curriculum.

1 Muslim students reported that they felt more 'successful' in Ancient History lessons than in other history topics. The majority of students also rated highly their 'success'.
    For the purpose of this research, success is measured in terms of academic attainment, knowledge retention, intellectual curiosity and engagement with learning. Quantitative data from the questionnaires indicated that 76 per cent of Muslim respondents agreed that they felt successful in their Ancient History lessons, only six per cent of Muslim students said they strongly disagreed with this idea. Furthermore, 60 per cent of Muslim respondents agreed that they felt more successful in these Ancient Middle East lessons than they did in other topics that they studied in Year Nine

(McOmish 2021). Although 30 per cent said they neither agreed nor disagreed with this second element of success, very small proportions, 6.2 per cent and 3.3 per cent, respectively, said they 'somewhat' or 'strongly' disagreed with this idea (McOmish 2021).

Responses from the interviews contextualised this finding. When explaining why they felt these ideas of success, Muslim interviewees expressed an appreciation of the fact that this topic was (a) outside of Europe and (b) was different from commonly taught topics that they felt disconnected from and bored by, such as the World Wars. A Black male Muslim student asserted in an interview that he appreciated the geographical diversity of the Ancient History topic because, *'What already I've learned so far in school has so far just been European countries, European countries, but not different countries like Eastern countries and stuff'*.

Qualitative data illustrated that Muslim students defined being successful in lessons as retaining good historical knowledge and academic achievement. An Asian male Muslim student (the same learner who provided the exceptional assessment discussed above) asserted that it was in studying the Ancient Middle East that he felt he had come into his own in terms of academic success. When asked if he felt successful in lessons he stated:

> Yeah, because I actually find it interesting because since, since Year Eight, that's when I started focusing in History because I liked the topics. Cause now I'll get 'masterings' mainly. In boring topics in Year Seven I'd get mainly "developings".

It was a topic he came back to again, proudly reminding me that *'I think I got my first "Excelling", here in that topic!'*.[6]

Therefore, it is fair to conclude that for the majority of Muslim respondents and interviewees in this small-scale action-research study, being taught the history of the Ancient Middle East facilitated feelings of success in lessons. Interviews highlighted that it was the focus on non-European history that increased engagement, led to the retention of knowledge and boosted feelings of success.

2 Muslim students felt a greater sense of connection and belonging in lessons, when learning about the Ancient Middle East.

Interview responses suggested that Muslim students felt a sense of connection and belonging to this Ancient History unit. As part of semi-structured interviews, all interviewees were questioned on (a) what might make them feel connected to a topic and

(b) whether they did indeed feel a connection in this way to this Ancient Middle East topic. Muslim students repeatedly expressed that they did feel connection and that this was a result of either the geographical proximity of their personal background to the area, or a direct familial connection to the area. An Asian female Muslim student explained that it was due to her family hailing from Pakistan that she felt greater interest in the topic:

> 'My family's from Pakistan.... Because I could relate to it more. It was more interesting because I get to know more'.

Similarly, an Asian male Muslim student argued that he felt a greater sense of connection to the topic because of his belief that he held heritage from the area:

> '...everyone migrates from one place to another, and as it's close to my home country, Pakistan, it seems likely... possibly I inherited heritage from Iraq or Syria'.

Another Asian male Muslim student explained that his sense of connection stemmed from the fact that his own family originated from nearby areas of the Middle East, which added a greater sense of value for him:

> 'I felt like a connection...'cause I am from that kind of ethnic background. So like it's good to learn about your background in that way. Like, some of the history where you come from and what you think about it'.

Interestingly, as well as ethnic connections to the area fostering a sense of belonging within the topic, students also reflected upon how their Islamic faith helped build that sense of connection too. A Black male Muslim student reflected on their own learning at Mosque and stated that:

> 'Because I'm Muslim, and I understand that the Middle East is mostly Muslim. I go to Mosque and we learn a lot about what's going on in the Middle East, about Islam, how history has helped in Islam. I understand a bit'.

These responses demonstrate that for the Muslim students interviewed, studying the ancient history of the Middle East engendered a greater sense of connection and belonging in their lessons and curriculum. Our experiences at Aldridge show that teaching Ancient History facilitates the creation of an inclusive curriculum, rather than an exclusionary, elitist one.

3 Black students were highly positive about, and engaged by, the topic.

The responses of Black students were not an area that this research sought to focus on at its inception. However, the quantitative and the qualitative data supplied by Black students was so positive that it would be remiss not to consider it a significant finding of this research and an important point to consider regarding the expansion of Classics. Overall, 84 per cent of Black African, 100 per cent of Black Caribbean and 75 per cent of White and Black Caribbean students all agreed that 'studying the topic gave me respect for the history of the Middle East' (McOmish 2021). Furthermore, Black students indicated that they felt successful in their lessons on the Ancient Middle East: 85 per cent of Black African, 100 per cent of Black Caribbean, and 100 per cent of Black Caribbean and White students agreed they felt successful in lessons (McOmish 2021). Overall, on these questions, Black students had higher percentages of positive responses than their White and Muslim counterparts.

This finding was further contextualised by the interview data. During interviews, Black African students (both Christian and Muslim) consistently discussed their interest in the topic, how they felt knowledgeable in the history they were learning and how much they enjoyed the learning process. The interview data also helped explain why Black students responded so positively: when asked about a sense of belonging and connection, Black students had a tendency to say that the topic felt (a) geographically closer to areas they consider representative of themselves, and (b) it felt like a difference and a change from Eurocentric topics that dominate the curriculum. A Black male Christian student said that he felt a greater sense of connection to this topic because of how it was removed from a European sphere of focus and closer towards regions he felt more personally connected to, which he broadly referred to as 'Africa':

> 'The Middle East is of course, like it's closer to home, like Africa in general. So like it seems more diverse than when we just talked about like fairly British and European things, like Vikings and so on'.

It seemed that Black students appreciated studying history that was geographically and ethnically diverse and they felt more connected to this than commonly taught European history such as Medieval Kings and the World Wars. It is important here to state that students were not hyper-critical of areas of European focus within the curriculum: in the same conversation where they emphasised their enjoyment of non-European history they would also assert the importance of the European history they did study. However, they were clearly engaged with content that encompassed global or world history. Therefore, teaching the Ancient Middle East had a positive impact on the Black students in this study, giving these students a greater connection to the topic, as well as a greater sense of success in lessons. If we are considering the role of Classics in the KS3 curriculum, it seems clear that adopting a study of the Ancient Middle East has been a productive step in creating a curriculum that better involves and engages Black students from a range of ethnic backgrounds at Aldridge School.

4 Ancient History holds particular value among students because it helps them to understand causation and consequence in human history.

One of the important effects of teaching Ancient History is how it actively bolsters learners' understanding of the historical concepts of causation and consequence. This was demonstrated through two sub-findings: (a) how far students could see similarities between Ancient History and more recent history, and (b) how far the topic helped students see how humanity has developed to the modern day. This was particularly exemplified by students' awareness of the development of empires, and the impact and personality of leaders (where they compared Middle Eastern kings to Medieval counterparts).

An Asian female Muslim student clearly identified understanding empire building as an area that made Ancient History particularly valuable. When asked how far the topic felt different from others studied, she responded:

> '…because it was ancient, how it built up upon the empire was interesting and excites me, and it makes me curious about what happened before. And Ancient History takes you to what happened before'. She later commented: 'I want to know how we got to the empires we have now and to do that Ancient History is a good way to see'.

The second theme highlighted by students was how they valued Ancient History because of how it explained human development and their understanding of causation and consequence. An Asian female Muslim student explained how she was especially influenced by the work of the Assyrians in this regard:

'...like the library (of Nineveh), if they didn't build it who knows what would have happened, when they started teaching people to read and write, maybe that wouldn't have happened without the library'.

Students felt that in studying the Ancient Middle East they accessed a deeper and broader understanding of societal progression than with a KS3 curriculum that began in CE 1066. Ancient History has, therefore, been shown to form a valuable and relevant part of the KS3 curriculum, recognised by students. Far from the topic being confusing because of its chronological distance from Modern History and the standard progression of a linear KS3 curriculum, students were able to compare and contrast thematic ideas across vast time periods and slot new schema into their already established knowledge of human development.

Limitations of the study

There are, of course, limitations to this study and what it can 'prove'. This research was undertaken with a relatively small group of students, who were asked about their responses to the topic around eight months after they had studied it. This was not ideal; the closure of schools from January 2021 to March 2021 significantly delayed data gathering. Additionally, this research was conducted at only one school, and although it does have ethnic and religious diversity, the findings based on religious identity would be better tested on larger cohorts. It would be interesting to see the results of teaching this same unit at schools with different socio-economic demographics, e.g. in a rural location, or in a school where BAME students are the majority to see if similar responses were generated. Unfortunately, this was beyond the scope of this study.

Furthermore, there were some areas of the initial questionnaire that students struggled with which thus impacted the quantitative data, for example, the meaning of 'connection' and 'belonging'. Upon interviewing students, it became clear that many did not have the emotional literacy to correctly understand what those words meant in this context and instead guessed at them meaning 'understanding' and a 'comfortability' with the topic. If more students had had this question explained to them before taking the questionnaire, or more had understood the terms in their context, the quantitative data may have matched more closely with the compelling qualitative data found in the interviews. As it was, the qualitative data cleared up misunderstandings and solidified findings.

Recommendations for professional practice and policy

1 Ancient History can play a valuable role in the KS3 curriculum, facilitating a deeper and more nuanced understanding of historical themes and skills.

   Many History teachers assume that disrupting the chronology of their curriculum would be confusing for students, undermining their understanding of the past. For teachers looking to include Ancient History or Classical Civilisation in their curriculum, I make two key recommendations. Firstly, make the break in chronology clear and well-explained, as outlined above, and, secondly, link this teaching to the wider curriculum thematically.

   To support students in understanding the relevance of the Ancient History topic, key themes should be established in the topic that are developed in multiple areas of the curriculum. This allows students to develop an understanding of the longevity and significance of themes in human history, facilitates building historical skills, such as understanding causation and consequence, and encourages the ability to critically compare historical periods. This Ancient Middle East unit investigated key themes such as imperialism, monarchy/leadership, societal/cultural development, warfare and human rights, all of which are present in multiple units across the KS3 curriculum. This tied content together thematically, not simply in terms of chronological development.

2 Teaching of the Ancient Middle East should be incorporated into the KS3 curriculum as an effective means to improve the inclusion of Asian history in the KS3 curriculum.

   An important question for educators, and especially those from majority ethnic backgrounds, is how often are we teaching periods of history that include cultures completely outside the sphere of European influence/involvement? In this research, it was remarkable how often Muslim Asian and Muslim/Christian Black students remarked (positively) that this Ancient Middle East unit was not European history. One of the most important elements of this unit, which contributed towards such high levels of connection and sense of success in Muslim students and Black students, is how it is entirely focused on the agency and power of the Middle East without studying this region in the context of what it meant for Europe/Britain. The topic looked at events and dynasties in terms of what they meant for the development of Ancient History in the Middle East and, in so doing, emphasised the significance and autonomy of the area. Studying the Ancient Middle East at Aldridge School supported the genuine, positive inclusion of Asian Muslim and Black Muslim students in the KS3 curriculum; it tackled the threat of an 'absent curriculum' and gave students a more global perspective on the past.

Conclusion

This unit, of course, was not a study of Islamic history – the content covered predates the advent of Islam by some 1000 years. However, it was our hope that by studying geographical regions that relate to the origins of Islam and modern-day Islamic populations, Muslim students would feel better represented in their KS3 curriculum. The responses collected suggest this was indeed the case. Teaching the Ancient Middle East at KS3 fostered a sense of success in the Muslim students in the study, as they reported feeling engaged in the lessons and able to succeed academically. The topic also engendered feelings of connection and belonging in the curriculum through familial connections to the areas studied and helped them to make thematic links across KS3 units. Black students, both Muslim and Christian, also engaged very positively with these topics. They emphasised the significance of history that operates outside of the European sphere of influence.

It is important to note that data relating to White students, although they were not the focus of this study, also demonstrated positive engagement with the unit. Over 62 per cent of White students agreed that it had given them respect for new areas of history, and 82 per cent of White students said that they now understood the achievements of the Ancient Middle East (McOmish 2021). Moreover, when asked what they enjoyed about the topic, 51 per cent said they enjoyed studying a period of history very different to their own background and 62 per cent said they enjoyed studying a period of history far removed from modern Britain (McOmish 2021). Teaching the Ancient Middle East was purposeful and engaging for the ethnically, socially and economically diverse students included in this study. It formed a meaningful and productive part of a diverse KS3 curriculum, and most importantly for this study, improved the provision of inclusive history for all students. I believe that Ancient History is set for expansion in the state-maintained sector as schools across Britain look to adapt and improve the range and diversity of their History teaching.

Notes

1. The Index of Multiple Deprivation is the official measure of deprivation for small areas of England.
2. Changes were made in 2017 which revised A-Level Ancient History and Classical Civilisation subject content. AS Levels were decoupled, meaning that all assessments became linear: AS could be taken after one year, or A-Level after two years.
3. Changes to the GCSE grading system in 2014 meant that grades allotted ranged from U (ungraded) to 9.
4. BAME is a problematic term, as highlighted in a recent government report (https://www.ethnicity-facts-figures.service.gov.uk/style-guide/writing-about-ethnicity), however when this research was conducted the term was used in school policy at Aldridge to reflect the diverse student body discussed in this chapter.
5. This research was undertaken as a Master of Arts qualification at the University of Birmingham, where ethical approval was granted. Participation in the study was optional, consent could be withdrawn at any time.
6. Within the school's KS3 marking policy students can attain one of the following five levels in assessments: Initial > Developing > Secure > Mastering > Excelling.

Reference List

Bourke, S. 2008. *The Middle East: The Cradle of Civilization Revealed.* London: Thames and Hudson Ltd.

Bruner, J. S. 1960. *The Process of Education.* Cambridge, MA: Harvard University Press.

Connolly, E. 2019. *Deprivation in Walsall: Summary Report.* Walsall: Economy and Environment, Walsall Council.

Connolly, L. 2013. *2011 Census Reports. Key Statistics for Walsall: Borough Summary.* Walsall: Walsall Council.

Department for Education. 2019. *Aldridge School – A Science College.* Accessed 11 August 2021. https://www.compare-school-performance.service.gov.uk/school/137974/aldridge-school—a-science-college/absence-and-pupil-population.

Ireland, J. and M. Mouthaan. 2020. "Perspectives on curriculum design: comparing the spiral and the network models". *Research Matters: A Cambridge Assessment Publication* 30: 7–12.

McOmish, A. 2021. "'I got my first excelling!': a study of the responses of Islamic students to the inclusion of Ancient Middle Eastern history at KS3". MA dissertation, The University of Birmingham.

Whitburn, R. and S. Yemoh. 2012. "'My people struggled too': hidden histories and heroism – A school-designed, post-14 course on multi-cultural Britain since 1945." *Teaching History*. 147: 16–24. Accessed 11 August 2021. http://www.jstor.org/stable/43260807.

Wilkinson, M.L.N. 2014a. "The concept of the absent curriculum: The case of the Muslim contribution and the English National Curriculum for history". *The Journal of Curriculum Studies* 46 (4): 419–444. Accessed 11 August 2021. https://doi.org/10.1080/00220272.2013.869838.

Wilkinson, M.L.N. 2014b. "Helping Muslim boys succeed: The case for history education". *The Curriculum Journal* 25 (3): 396–431. Accessed 11August 2021. https://doi.org/10.1080/09585176.2014.929527.

Walsall Council. 2011. *2011 Census: Walsall Ward Profiles*. Accessed 11 August 2021. https://go.walsall.gov.uk/Portals/0/images/importeddocuments/census_2011_aldridge_central_south_profile.pdf.

6 Whose museum is it anyway?

Connecting with communities at the Museum of Classical Archaeology, Cambridge

Susanne Turner

The Museum

The Museum of Classical Archaeology (MOCA) in Cambridge is a small university museum. Of the nine University of Cambridge Museums (UCM) which receive funding from Arts Council England as a National Portfolio Organisation (NPO), MOCA is the smallest.[1] The Museum's purpose-built Cast Gallery is nestled inside the Faculty of Classics building and houses a collection of more than 600 plaster casts of classical sculpture. It is one of three major surviving collections of plaster casts in the UK today – and the only one of the three which sits outside a major museum.[2]

Plaster casts are a tricky kind of object. As replicas, they collapse the distinctions we like to make between different time periods and functions, so that they might carry meaning for viewers as *both* ancient object *and* Victorian reproduction, as *both* artistic inspiration *and* teaching aid (Whitehead 2009). Mary Beard, writing when she was Curator of MOCA in the 1990s, has shown how these very contradictions and ambivalences fuelled furious debates around the status of the Cambridge cast collection in the last quarter of the nineteenth century and first decades of the twentieth century and also shaped its future (Beard 1994).[3]

This is all to say that, like many small university museums in the UK (and, perhaps especially, dedicated classical archaeology collections), MOCA houses a specialist and slightly esoteric collection. But who is this collection for, today? To whom does a university collection like MOCA's belong – or, perhaps better, who belongs within a university museum? University museums are not embedded in their communities or localities as are their local and regional counterparts; their visitors are unlikely to be coming because of a shared sense of inherited identity or history embodied by the collection or its sense

DOI: 10.4324/9781003181958-7

Whose museum is it anyway? 91

of place. University museums instead might be understood to build their own communities based around shared subject-specialist interests, whether within the university itself (e.g., the student body, whose access might be facilitated by teaching within the collection) or dispersed beyond its walls, both globally and locally.

It has, however, long been clear that labelling MOCA as simply a teaching collection does not capture the full range of the Museum's audiences today. A quick glance at the annual visitor figures (pre-pandemic) is revealing.[4] MOCA attracts 13,000–15,000 visitors per year. Of these, only around 15 per cent are using the Cast Gallery for university teaching, primarily members of the Faculty of Classics; a further c.30 per cent of those visitors are coming on school visits or participating in outreach activities. The rest – c.55 per cent – are either general visitors or are attending specific events. These figures suggest that the cast collection is no longer 'just' a teaching collection – rather, visitors come for a multitude of reasons which go beyond facilitated learning at either university or school level.

There are, however, very real barriers to access for non-university members considering a visit to MOCA. Access to the Museum is not only restricted by mundane practicalities like opening hours and location but is also notably delimited by the rhythms of university life. MOCA is easier to access for those who have free time during the week: weekend opening is restricted to Saturdays, and only those Saturdays which fall within the University of Cambridge's term-time. MOCA can also be decidedly difficult to find, since it has no entrance on the road and there is limited wayfinding signage. Visitors must negotiate entry to an unmarked university site and come into a university building, passing a university library and university teaching rooms, before finding the museum at the top of the stairs. Threshold anxiety is a very real concern, and visitors who are not already well-acquainted with the university may feel that they are not welcome or do not belong in unfamiliar university buildings; these feelings, moreover, are likely to impact visitors from some backgrounds more than others.[5] Non-members of the University, in other words, may sometimes feel that determination is a key characteristic required to enter the Museum.

In what follows, I want to explore how at MOCA we have engaged communities beyond both the University and the wider world of classical studies – and thus tried to expand the museum's reach and, by extension, expand access to the classical past – and to touch on what is at stake when we do.[6] Over recent years, the core staff of three at MOCA have developed a range of strategies to try to overcome the barriers to access outlined above, and to engage, welcome, or tempt in different audiences who are neither connected to the University nor harbour a specialist interest in Classics as a discipline. Some of this work is supported by the UCM and in turn supports the UCM's wider mission and key priorities as an NPO. Crucially, the strategies we have developed are commensurate to our relatively limited resources and small size – and also build on the particular strengths and idiosyncrasies of our collection.

Creative communities

In the introduction to the exhibition catalogue for the 2018 exhibition *The Classical Now*, a show which explored the power that classical models continue to hold over artists today, Michael Squire wrote of how it is the possibilities which Ancient Greek and Roman sculptures embody *in the present* which enthrals: 'for all their pastness, however, these objects also have a presence, whether as ideal, antitype or point of departure' (Squire 2018, xii). Through programming which focuses on the creative potential embodied by the casts, at MOCA we have discovered that this statement is as true of audiences as it is of artists – and, indeed, that these two categories can overlap in productive ways.

In May 2015, a new event was trialled at MOCA which went on to become a key part of the Museum's summer programming: *Drink and Draw*. The aim was to create a relaxed and informal evening of sketching and unpressured creative expression. MOCA provided drawing materials and a glass of wine (or a non-alcoholic alternative) – and engaged the services of professional artists, who were on hand to offer light-touch artistic guidance to those who wanted such instruction. Attendees simply needed to tie a ribbon to their chair to indicate that they would like some help.

Drink and Draw events had gained popularity in the UK at around the same time, usually on a relatively small scale and often focused on life-drawing, where attendees might be nervous when faced with a naked model for the first time (Buist 2015). MOCA's event was different, on a larger scale and with the nudity provided by the casts. On the night, *Drink and Draw* proved to be both more popular and larger in scale than we could have anticipated when we proposed the idea: a queue soon wove around the University site when the Cast Gallery hit capacity. Inside, the atmosphere was buoyant and tranquil, as participants hunched quietly over their clipboards to create their own masterpieces.

Drink and Draw has since grown to be one of the keystone events in the Museum calendar – regularly requested, talked about and invariably well attended (Thornber 2018a, 2020, 142–143). It now runs twice a year in the summer months, once in May and once in August, when the light is good and the weather is kinder on queuing outside. Feedback is always positive and indicates that many attendees are first-time visitors, discovering the Museum and its collection for the first time through an event with an artistic focus rather than one with a strictly didactic or classically minded aim. Feedback forms frequently cite the relaxed atmosphere, evening timing outside regular opening hours, and opportunity for creative inspiration and expression as particular strengths. The requested improvements include requests for more wine (since consumption is limited to one glass per person, to keep the focus on the artistic activity), or for more frequent sessions.

Drink and Draw, therefore, attracts an audience which seeks out the casts as objects of artistic inspiration, rather than only as simulacra of archaeological artefacts – and, in doing so, it taps into a longstanding conceptual triangulation amongst plaster casts, classical sculpture and art education. When the Museum of Classical and General Archaeology (as MOCA was originally named) threw open its doors on 6 May 1884, the speakers at the grand opening party framed the new museum as much as an aesthetic space as an educational one (Beard 1994, 1–2). Some of the great artists of the day were in attendance, including Sir Frederick Leighton and Lawrence Alma-Tadema. Plaster casts – valorised both for their whiteness and for their ability to capture the form of sculpture without the distractions of the original's materiality – had long been a mainstay of a formal fine art education.[7] From the seventeenth century onwards, collections of plaster casts in fine art schools functioned as surrogates for the classical models which students were required to study before they might progress to drawing or painting flesh-and-blood models.[8] *Drink and Draw*, in some sense, inherits this tradition while expanding access to both the museum and to classical art.

Contemporary exhibitions

Over the course of the twentieth century, however, the classical tradition loosened its grip on art students and plaster casts fell out of fashion as sources of inspiration and emulation, leading to the disbanding and destruction of the collections of casts held by many of the smaller art schools. Nonetheless, artists have continued to engage imaginatively with the classical past – in and through casts.[9] Lorenz Winkler-Horaček, curator of the Abguss-Sammlung Antiker Plastik in Berlin, has spoken eloquently of the ways in which plaster cast collections can come to life when paired with exhibitions of contemporary art (Winkler-Horaček 2016). Today, MOCA hosts up to three exhibitions a year in the Cast Gallery. By collaborating with artists, both local and international, we are able to create dialogues across past and present art practice – and perhaps go some way towards reframing the casts once again as art objects in their own right.

The most effective temporary exhibitions transform the space in unexpected ways. Loukas Morley's *The Silence of Time* in 2019, for instance, not only juxtaposed the abstraction of his works made from locally sourced salvaged materials with the figural forms of the casts but also used carefully placed mirrors to 'fold' the Cast Gallery back on itself. *Goddesses*, by New Zealand lithographer Marian Maguire, borrowed figures from Greek vase painting to reimagine the Olympian goddesses revaluating their traditional roles with a decidedly feminist slant: Athena is shown throwing away her weapons, Hera walking away from the trappings of her marriage, Aphrodite swapping men for self-improvement (see Maguire 2017; Stafford 2020). Norwich-born artist James Epps, supported by a *Developing Your Creative Practice* grant from Arts Council England, created a series of abstract interventions which wove around the casts like brightly coloured wall mosaics in 2021's *A twist of the hand*. MOCA's collaborations with artists are, in other words, varied – and each encourages visitors (often surprised by the startling presence of contemporary art) to look afresh at the casts through a different lens.

Temporary exhibitions also allow MOCA to expand its collaboration with the local artistic community in a tangible way. Nowhere is the social impact of this support more evident than in an ongoing partnership between the Museum and Cambridge Community Arts (CCA), an inspiring local organisation which runs an ever-growing number of creative courses designed to improve mental health and reduce social isolation. For four years, MOCA has been hosting an annual exhibition of work by the learners on CCA's photography course. The goal is that their learners master not only the technical elements of how to use a camera or edit photographs but also how to express themselves creatively. Moreover, the ultimate aim of CCA's courses is empowerment: learners are supported once the course ends not only to continue to pursue their creativity but also to move on to further education or employment.

Each year, at the end of their course, the photography learners select their favourite images for display in a celebratory exhibition. Some will be images of MOCA's casts, taken on an earlier research trip; others might be of objects in our sister collections, or locations invested with personal significance to the learners themselves.[10] MOCA provides the space and the audience – but most importantly, we host an evening Private View in the Cast Gallery where all learners can enjoy their exhibition after hours with their friends and family. The learners and their families come from a range of backgrounds; many might never be emboldened to cross the threshold of the Museum if not for this celebration. Their feedback indicates that the hosting of their work in a public museum is a particularly important milestone for them (Thornber 2017; Turner 2020).

For CCA's learners, their engagement with MOCA's collection is one stopping point, if a significant one, on a journey of personal discovery; the casts have less meaning for them as embodiments of the classical past than they do as awe-inspiring mainstays of the art world. This is a welcome reminder that the continuing relevance of our collections can only be found in the present day and is bound up as much in their sheer potential for meaning to different visitors as in their historicity – and that, even as university collections, we need not necessarily focus on the latter at the expense of the former.

LGBTQ+ communities

Interpretation in museums is important. Labels and interpretation panels inform visitors about the museum's objects, giving them a starting point from which to make sense of a collection and putting individual objects in relation to each other as well as to a broader context beyond the artefacts themselves. Museums tell stories about their objects and, in order for those stories to make sense, they tend to create what Eilean Hooper-Greenhill calls 'master narratives' (Hooper-Greenhill 2000, 4). Those master narratives, as they are told through permanent displays, are notoriously slow to change – and they necessarily privilege some stories over others. Labels are not often updated as the winds of academic study or of wider society change course (Siapkas and Sjörgen 2014). The impact of this tendency towards interpretative inertia in museums, however, is that some audiences can feel unrepresented (and, correspondingly, unwelcome) in our collections because we are not telling inclusive stories or inclusive histories (Heimlich and Koke 2013).

Queer Antiquities

Queer Antiquities, a hand-trail and accompanying series of small interpretation panels launched to coincide with LGBTQ+ History Month in February 2018, was part of an effort at MOCA to make space for more of those stories which we were not otherwise telling. Scholarship (and popular culture) has long been interested in what today might be called homoerotic or queer relationships and identities in the

Graeco-Roman past.[11] But, as in many museums, the 'master narrative' of the Cast Gallery did not make much, if any, space for the history of homosexuality.[12] MOCA's Gallery is purpose-built to arrange the casts in a broadly chronological layout and, as a result, the permanent labels (last redeveloped in 2009) tend to favour more traditional art historical interpretation of classical sculpture. There are not only real advantages to this floorplan – visitors who know very little about classical art are empowered to, quite literally, see for themselves the types of changes which take place in the sculpting of the human body over a period of around 1000 years – but there are also obvious limitations.

Queer Antiquities was therefore designed to be highly visible, creating space for LGBTQ+ stories in the Gallery. The bright and colourful hand-trail was written with a light tone and leads visitors on a journey around the Museum through a selection of nine objects, spotlighting LGBTQ+ stories both ancient and modern – ranging from the tale of the Tyrannicides, Harmodius and Aristogeiton in Athens, to Winckelmann's affection for the Apollo Belvedere, to Hercules' swapping of gender identities with Omphale. The addition of interpretation panels not only expanded the detailed content but also increased visibility: in practice, many visitors came across the panels rather than picking up the hand-trail.

The trail was so positively received that the interpretation panels remained in place until October 2021 and the hand-trail has never been taken out of circulation, now effectively forming a permanent addition to the Cast Gallery and on its fourth printing. A student recently told us that seeing the trail made him feel 'seen and accepted': this type of representation of LGBTQ+ history *as history* matters. However, unsurprisingly, *Queer Antiquities* does not work for all visitors, and there is certainly room for improvement. The greater visibility of male same-sex desire in the ancient past and its visual culture, for instance, means that female same-sex desire gets only the briefest of mentions.[13] Moreover, *Queer Antiquities* very much represents a top-down model of museum interpretation, produced by MOCA's small team entirely in-house – none of whom identified as LGBTQ+. Although it was produced at the suggestion of, and in consultation with, a volunteer who does identify as LGBTQ+, *Queer Antiquities* nonetheless very much remains a curatorial or institutional museum voice on LGBTQ+ histories.

Bridging Binaries

In contrast, another project launched by the UCM one year later mobilised a bottom-up model of interpretation. *Bridging Binaries* saw volunteer-led LGBTQ+ tours introduced to the galleries of four of the museums towards the end of 2018, including at MOCA in time for LGBTQ+ History Month in February 2019 (Bull and Hughes 2018; Bull et al. 2019; Bull and Hughes 2020). Three further collections were added to the programme later in 2019. Dan Vo, a freelance consultant who founded the Victoria and Albert Museum's award-winning volunteer-led LGBTQ tours, and Eleanor Armstrong, a freelance science communicator who ran the tour series *Queering the Science Museum*, collaborated with curators across the museums to produce the content – but the volunteers make that content their own, weaving their own (often personal and personalised) take on LGBTQ+ stories in and through our collections. In MOCA, that might mean using a sculpture of Aphrodite to talk about the articulation of female desire in Sappho's poetry or using the figure of Caeneus on the frieze from the Temple of Apollo at Bassae to think about gender change and fluidity in the ancient world. Volunteer guides have chosen to think through ancient sculpture and culture via a broad range of contemporary LGBTQ+ and queer frames, including but not limited to asexuality, bisexuality and trans identities, depending partly on their own positioning or identification/s – and also strikingly going beyond the limitations of *Queer Antiquities* noted above.

Multivocality is therefore a key component of the *Bridging Binaries* project. The aim is to diversify the museum voice; that is, to bring in fresh or otherwise unheard perspectives and to expand beyond the traditional and institutional voices of academics and museum staff. This might seem like a laudable but potentially challenging approach in a university museum, where the desire to provide an authoritative and trustworthy source of information on the collections in our care can perhaps shade all too easily into gatekeeping (that is, overly dictating how the collection is viewed and perceived). Yet, projects like *Bridging Binaries* can demonstrate in powerful ways how multiple and different modes of interpretation can productively coexist. The volunteer tour guides are supported as they find their own voices (e.g. Clews 2020). They undertake an extensive preparatory programme of training, have opportunities to consult with museum staff on their chosen content and are also encouraged to engage in their own research.

Museum Remix

Multivocality and community consultation is also central to *Museum Remix*, an annual UCM project which seeks to radically rethink collections. Over the years, *Museum Remix* has taken many different forms.[14] In 2019, the focus was on the LGBTQ+ stories showcased in the *Bridging Binaries* tours: several groups of museum activists were invited to reconceptualise how five UCM, including MOCA, engage with those LGBTQ+ histories through artistic intervention. The resulting artworks would be put on show in a one-night-only exhibition with a focus on themes of love, sex and censorship.[15]

MOCA's team chose to focus on the stories of Caracalla and Hermaphroditus (I am consciously using Hermaphroditus as god and capitalised, to avoid the stigmatising connotations which cling to the word 'hermaphrodite'; see Dreger et al. 2005). The case of Hermaphroditus, in particular, is a striking example of how untold stories can come about through absence rather than presence in museum collections: in 1849–1850, the Fitzwilliam Museum was offered a plaster cast of a Hermaphroditus but turned it down, swapping it out for another cast.[16] The long-term impact of this decision is that, to this day, the MOCA's cast collection does not include a Hermaphroditus. The team engaged thoughtfully with this absence, negotiating the potential for the fetishisation of the intersex body by crafting a version of the Sleeping Hermaphroditus in the Louvre from air-dry clay – and, keenly aware of the lack of intersex representation in their group, they added a mirror in place of genitalia, to catch out the viewer's objectifying gaze. At the end of January 2019, MOCA's Remix team helped to install their works in the Cast Gallery, complete with new labels and an interactive display asking visitors to respond with further stories they would like to see told in the space (Knott et al. 2020).

Bridging Binaries and *Museum Remix* are large-scale, ambitious projects, conceptually as well as logistically: our membership of the UCM empowers MOCA to participate in projects and pursue goals which might otherwise be out of our reach as a small museum. When the *Bridging Binaries* volunteers introduce their tour members to the museum, they are asked to remind visitors that they are 'accepted, respected and welcome' in our museums, and that 'we seek to provide a safe space for non-binary, non-heteronormative stories to be shared and give a platform to a minority voice – of the community, and for the community'. By making our work engaging the LGBTQ+ community a very visible part of our programming, we have taken that sentiment to heart (Shoulder and Small 2020).

Connecting communities

Minimus Primary Latin Project

So far, I have focused on projects which are intended to bring specific communities of people united by shared identities or interests into the

Whose museum is it anyway? 99

museum. Now, I want to turn to a project which instead brings the study of the classical world – and the classicists who study it – out of the museum or university and into the community. In 2013, MOCA launched a volunteer project which was intended to create connections across the university-locality divide: the *Minimus* Primary Latin Project (Thornber 2018b). As part of this project, our students, both undergraduate and postgraduate, take the fruits of their studies out into local state-maintained primary schools, where they deliver after-school Latin clubs using the popular and successful *Minimus* Latin course, published by Cambridge University Press (Bell 1999; Bell and Wing-Davey 2018).

In 2013, we began by partnering with two schools and with six volunteers. Today, we work with four schools – although in pre-pandemic years, that number has been as high as six. Since the project began, over 100 student volunteers have run 33 Latin Clubs in local primary schools, and over 350 local school children have taken part. In keeping with the tone of the *Minimus* books, the aim is not to provide dry and dull schooling in Latin vocabulary and grammar, but rather to use Latin as a gateway to explore the culture and history of Rome beyond just its language – and to do so in a way which is fun, light-hearted and not too onerous, given that the children have already spent a full day in school. And yet, it might seem rather odd for a museum to run a programme which has little to no grounding in its collection or objects: why bother?

Leaving aside the many benefits for children learning Latin (Bracke and Bradshaw 2020; Holmes-Henderson 2021; Holmes-Henderson and Kelly 2022), one of the great strengths of a university museum is the knowledge, experience and skills of the academics and student body on its very doorstep. It makes sense for MOCA to function as a gateway to the Faculty of Classics for the public, mobilising this embarrassment of intellectual riches and goodwill in the form of lectures and lunchtime talks for public audiences on a broad range of ancient-world-related topics – most especially during the University-wide events intended to platform current research, such as the Alumni Festival in the autumn or the Cambridge Festival in the spring. But it also makes sense for us to lean into the strengths of our students, especially those who are eager to expand access to Classics in schools and who are all devoting so much of their time to learning ancient languages.[17] In the process, not only do we offer an opportunity to our students to learn new skills (foundations upon which many of our volunteers build by entering careers in education and outreach) but we also forge relationships between the university and the local community, between the Faculty and local primary schools, and (last but by no means least) between our student volunteers and the school children with whom they interact on a weekly basis during university term-time.

The student volunteers taking part in the *Minimus* Primary Latin Project are placed in groups and undertake training delivered by the Museum Education and Outreach Coordinator before they head out into the classroom, designed to empower them to create their own collaborative and imaginative lesson plans and resources. The volunteers are encouraged to think outside the educational box: Latin club sessions have been known to involve singing Latin songs (even with ukulele accompaniment), making mosaics, designing a Roman menu, dressing up in togas and responding creatively to (age-appropriate) Ancient Greek and Roman myths.[18] The aim is that they make learning Latin fun, rather than a chore. Perhaps unsurprisingly, they are also encouraged to include object-based learning in their planning, utilising images of a broad range of ancient artefacts as well as replica items from the Museum's teaching collection: oil lamps, wax tablets and even that perennial favourite – the sponge on a stick. In this way, the volunteers embed the children's understanding of the Latin language within a wider appreciation of the Roman world.

Running the *Minimus* Primary Latin Project is no small undertaking and represents a significant commitment for our small museum. Student volunteers are recruited in May to begin the project the following October; students are required to commit to the project for the full academic year, so the project also represents a meaningful commitment on their part. Over the summer months, each student undergoes a UK Disclosure and Barring Service check and, in the case of international students, an equivalent check in their country of residence. Before they start teaching in schools in October, the volunteers receive training in planning and delivering engaging sessions, behaviour management and safeguarding. Once the clubs are established, termly observations also take place so that the students can receive feedback.

In effect, the *Minimus* Primary Latin Project represents in microcosm the broader philosophy of MOCA that, just as the Cast Gallery is embedded within the Faculty of Classics, so too is the material and visual culture of the ancient past deeply embedded within its broader historical and cultural context. But more than that, it is also one of our most ambitious and embedded projects – and one which allows the Museum to support our own Faculty-focused community of students, the outreach efforts of the broader classics community and also the wider schools community in our local area. It is, in other words, so much more than just a simple Latin project.

Breaking Down Barriers

By way of conclusion, I would now like to consider two more recent projects, both of which continue to expand the types of histories we use MOCA's collection of nineteenth-century plaster casts to explore. In both of these projects, we have sought to bring out the contemporary relevance of our collection and the issues that Greek and Roman sculpture still raises for diverse audiences today.

Beyond the Pale

Beyond the Pale is a trail to bring colour to Classics: it uses the trail format first trialled in MOCA's *Queer Antiquities* to take visitors on a different journey through the Cast Gallery, one in which they might view Greek and Roman sculpture through the prism of polychromy. The passage of time, exposure to the elements and even invasive cleaning have combined to make the original pigments on ancient statues disappear from our collective view; but if the sculptures with which we are now so familiar were not colourless, we ask, what would it mean to see them with their colour restored? And how has the loss of so much original polychromy shaped how the classical past has been viewed over the centuries?

Installed in October 2021, the production of *Beyond the Pale* was more ambitious than *Queer Antiquities*. Eight large-scale interpretation panels tackle wide-ranging topics. This was never intended to be just a story of pigments and paint shadows, but one which asks visitors to consider the broader history and implications of viewing Greek and Roman sculpture as colourless. With this in mind, we recruited a panel of student volunteers to advise on content and help draft some of the panels. Consideration of race and imperialism is central to this broader, multivalent history: in relation to the Apollo Belvedere, for instance, we address the difficult history of 'facial angle theory', while four figurines of Black males from Naukratis from our reserve collection help us to address the diversity of both ancient societies and sculpture. Never before have these four objects been brought into dialogue with our casts by being put on public display.

Discussion of the Parthenon's polychromy and the politics of its cleaning leads to politics of a different kind as visitors are given the opportunity to vote on whether the Parthenon sculptures in the British Museum should remain in London or return to Athens – an issue which is under increasing scrutiny in the news at the time of writing. In this way, visitors are able to shape the impact of the trail in the

Gallery: after the first year, 109 votes had been cast for return compared to 61 for retention. Visitors will continue to vote while the trail is on display, but we hope the development of a printed hand trail and an online version will expand the accessibility of this project.

Go Figure!

A second project, currently under development, aims to have teenagers talk about body image, engaging them with MOCA's plaster casts of Greek and Roman sculpture through conversation about issues particularly high on their own agenda. *Go Figure!* is a partnership with the Advocating Classics Education (ACE) project and funded by the Arts and Humanities Research Council Follow-On Funding grant awarded to Dr Arlene Holmes-Henderson. We have modelled what we do on the methodology developed by the Sex and History team at the University of Exeter, a methodology grounded in using objects from the past not only to develop critical thinking but to create a safe space for talking about sensitive issues.

Working collaboratively with Alice Hoyle, a Relationships and Sex Education expert who helped to develop the Sex and History methodology, we are developing sessions which are aimed at teachers and teenagers who may have had little to no exposure to studying the classical world. Consultation sessions with young people and teachers have so far indicated that audiences are receptive to using ancient statues to talk about their bodies and how cultures, inherited and contemporary, shape how they see their bodies – and have also elicited an eagerness among younger audiences to find out more about the sculptures themselves (Figures 6.1 and 6.2). The aim is to produce sessions which can be delivered in a range of ways, facilitated either by museum staff in the Museum or online or by teachers themselves in the classroom.

Not an ending: looking forward, doing more

In this chapter, I have tried to show how – through a range of projects with partners and communities – a university museum like MOCA may be small but it can also be mighty. In the mission to engage audiences and promote interest in the classical world, the idiosyncrasies of our collections can be our greatest strength. In the case of MOCA, that means leaning into the creative histories of plaster casts as a category of object, the relevance of the rich untold (and too often untapped) stories of the ancient world to today's diverse audiences and the subject-specific skill-sets of our student body.

Whose museum is it anyway? 103

What affects young people's body image?

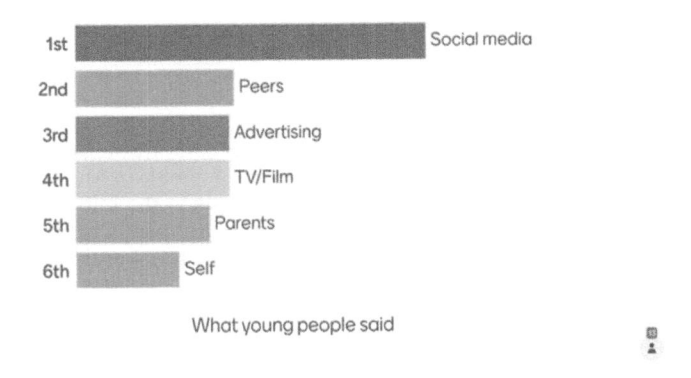

1st	██████████	Social media
2nd	████	Peers
3rd	████	Advertising
4th	██	TV/Film
5th	██	Parents
6th	██	Self

What young people said

Figure 6.1 Mentimeter presentation slide. The results of a poll exercise during a session with young people.

The aim is that our projects are not standalone, but they intersect and help MOCA to widen not only the stories that we tell about the classical world and its peoples but also the voices for which we make space. Our collection may be limited, but its potential is not. At its root, museum work – from curation to learning and beyond – is about creating connections across time and space or, to

How was this session for you?

abs-olutely amazing
intesting   surprising
fun   intellectual   enjoyable
informative
fascinating   interesting   educational
intriguing
butt-iful   eye-opening   engaging   vulvtastic

Figure 6.2 Mentimeter presentation slide. The feedback received after a session with young people.

put it another way, fostering relationships between both people and objects. The ways in which we do so need not be limited solely to traditional interpretation.

Notes

1 https://museums.cam.ac.uk/.
2 The two other major collections of plaster casts are housed in the Victoria and Albert Museum in London and the Ashmolean Museum in Oxford. There are other smaller collections of casts in the UK of varying sizes, including a sizeable collection in Edinburgh, split between the Edinburgh College of Art and the University of Edinburgh; see https://sites.eca.ed.ac.uk/casts/the-collection/.
3 For more on the early history of the casts in Cambridge, see Beard (2012), Vout (2015, 17–25), and Burn (2016, 67–69). For recent guidance on the status of replicas as historical objects in museum and heritage contexts, see https://replicas.stir.ac.uk/principles-and-guidance/.
4 Visitor figures are published as part of MOCA's annual reports, which can be accessed here: https://www.classics.cam.ac.uk/museum/about-us/governance.
5 The term 'threshold fear', now also known as 'threshold anxiety', was coined by Gurian (2005). More recently, see Parry et al. (2018).
6 It might be objected that I am using the word 'community' in a slightly unusual sense here. 'Community' is a loaded term in the museum sector and is not often used in the sense that I am using it here, to think about building communities beyond the university. More usually, it is used in the context of outreach work within the community living in the locality of the museum (who may or may not already feel invested in the museum and its collection), or in the sense of 'source communities', the peoples (or their descendants) from whose culture artefacts in the collection originated and who have a vested interest in their care, display and ownership.
7 On the collecting and use of plaster casts in fine art schools for the provision of an artistic education, see Wade (2018, 21–42); on the role of copying beyond art schools in fine art education, see Duro (1988). On the changing relationships between museums and art schools, see Blythe (2016).
8 On drawing after the antique, see Aymonino (2015). Drawing from the antique was an integral part of the South Kensington system of art education, created in the nineteenth century by Henry Cole; for an outline, see Turpin (1983). The South Kensington Museum (today the V&A) was also at the centre of the systems for the distribution of government-funded plaster cast purchases to art schools throughout the UK, through the workshop of Domenico Brucciani in London; see Wade (2018, 24–26). Compare Foster (2015), on the South Kensington Museum and the circulation of casts beyond art schools.
9 See, for instance, Cahill (2018) and Squire et al. (2018). For an evocative account of the continued affection for casts in fine art schools, see Stevens (2018–2019), on the loss of the Glasgow School of Art's casts in two fires

at the Mackintosh Building. On the destruction of casts in art schools in the twentieth century, see Allington (1997); Allington reflects on the role of plaster casts in his work in Allington and Cahill (2018).

10 Some of the variety and passion can be seen in the online exhibition which replaced 2021's show (cancelled due to the ongoing pandemic): https://www.museums.cam.ac.uk/story/wanderings-with-our-cameras/.

11 The scholarship on this topic is vast, but seminal works demonstrating the longevity of this interest in male same-sex relationships include Dover (1979), Halperin (1990) and Davidson (2007).

12 The British Museum, for instance, had recognised a similar gap in its interpretation with the launch of the 'Desire, love, identity: LGBTQ histories trail' in 2017 (see Frost 2021) and the earlier publication of Parkinson 2013. On the heteronormativity of museum master narratives more generally, see Tseliou (2013); cf. Frost (2013).

13 This is probably a broader problem, which goes beyond the Classical past: in a review of interpretative methods for presenting LGBTQ+ history in museums, Susan Ferentinos notes that these strategies still tend to privilege the perspectives of white, cisgender men (Ferentinos 2019).

14 In 2021, the most recent Museum Remix introduced the voices of the *Bridging Binaries* guides into the Gallery, following the pandemic-induced absence of the tours, in the form of labels with QR codes which could be scanned so that visitors could listen to them deliver pre-recorded LGBTQ+ content. Their voices can be heard at the following link, after selecting 'Museum Remix' from the list: https://www.museums.cam.ac.uk/discover.

15 Online exhibition: https://www.museums.cam.ac.uk/story/museumremix 2019/.

16 The Hermaphroditus was part of a large-scale donation from the collection of Sir George Wombwell, facilitated by Mr John Kirkpatrick of Trinity, see Beard (1994, 7–8) and Vout (2015, 17–25). We do not know which ancient statue of Hermaphroditus was replicated in the lost cast, or what happened to it once it was refused. The decision to turn down the offer of the Hermaphroditus should probably be contextualised within the didactic and moral imperatives of the newly opened Fitzwilliam Museum; on attitudes to the public, see Burn (2016, 63–67). Nonetheless, it demonstrates how deliberately exclusions can occur through historic collections development decisions – and how their impact can act in the present, to reinforce potentially damaging oversights in the contemporary world around us; cf. Greaves (2018).

17 The delivery of Latin learning to school-age pupils has become a mainstay of university-based Classics outreach, e.g. at Reading and Nottingham; at the latter, the delivery of Latin afterschool clubs is integrated into a university-wide primary-focused Learning Leaders programme. At Swansea, students can participate in a placement module for credit, where they undertake teaching and are assessed on the learning materials they produce (Maria Oikonomou, pers. comm.). On the bigger picture of classics outreach (beyond university recruitment), see Lovatt (2011).

18 On the value of mythology in supporting multiliteracies in primary age children, see Holmes-Henderson (2021).

Reference List

Allington, E. 1997. "Venus a go go, to go". In *Sculpture and Its Reproductions*, edited by A. Hughes and E. Ranftt, 152–167. London: Reaktion Books.

Allington, E and J. Cahill 2018. "Interview: Edward Allington". In *The Classical Now*, edited by M. Squire, J. Cahill and R. Allen, 91–95. Milton Keynes: Elephant Publishing.

Aymonino, A. 2015. "Nature perfected': the theory and practice of drawing after the antique". In *Drawn from the Antique: Artists and the Classical Ideal*, edited by A. Aymonino and A. Varick Lauder, 15–63. London: Sir John Soane's Museum.

Beard, M. 1994. "Casts and cast-offs: the origins of the Museum of Classical Archaeology". *Proceedings of the Cambridge Philological Society* 39: 1–29.

Beard, M. 2012. "Cambridge's "Shrine of the Muses": the display of classical antiquities in the Fitzwilliam Museum, 1848-1998". *Journal of the History of Collections* 24 (3): 289–308.

Bell, B. 1999. *Minimus: Starting out in Latin*. Cambridge: Cambridge University Press.

Bell, B and Z. Wing-Davey 2018. "Delivering Latin in primary schools". In *Forward with Classics: Languages in Schools and Communities*, edited by A. Holmes-Henderson, S. Hunt and M. Musié, 111–128. London: Bloomsbury.

Blythe, S. G. 2016. "Keeping good company: art schools and museums". In *Museums and Higher Education Working Together: Challenges and Opportunities*, edited by A. Boddington, J. Boys and C. Speight, 83–90. London: Routledge.

Bracke, E. and C. Bradshaw. 2020. "The impact of learning Latin on school pupils: a review of existing data". *The Language Learning Journal* 48 (2): 226–236.

Buist, E. 2015. "Drink and draw classes: art and alcohol can be a good mix". *The Guardian,* 10 January 2015.

Bull, J. and N. Hughes. 2018. "Coming soon: LGBTQ+ tours in Cambridge Museums." *UCM Collections in Action blog*. Accessed 14 September 2021. https://www.museums.cam.ac.uk/blog/2018/09/07/coming-soon-lgbtq-tours-in-cambridge-museums/.

Bull, J. and N. Hughes. 2020. "Bridging Binaries LGBTQ+ Tours – where are we now?" *UCM Collections in Action blog*. Accessed 14 September 2021. https://www.museums.cam.ac.uk/blog/2020/06/05/bridging-binaries-lgbtq-tours-where-are-we-now/

Bull, J, H. Price and N. Hughes. 2019. "Bridging Binaries: reflections on the pilot". *UCM Collections in Action blog*. Accessed 14 September 2021. https://www.museums.cam.ac.uk/blog/2019/05/22/bridging-binaries-reflections-on-the-pilot/.

Burn, L. 2016. *The Fitzwilliam Museum: A History*. London: I.B. Tauris.

Cahill, J. 2018. "The classical in the contemporary: Contemporary Art in Britain and its relationships with Graeco-Roman Antiquity". Unpublished PhD thesis, University of Cambridge.

Clews, C. 2020. "Hadrian, Antinous and Me". *UCM Collections in Action blog.* Accessed 15 September 2021. https://www.museums.cam.ac.uk/blog/2020/06/07/hadrian-antinous-and-me/.

Davidson, J. 2007. *The Greeks and Greek Love.* London: Weidenfeld & Nicolson.

Dover, K. 1979. *Greek Homosexuality.* London: Duckworth.

Dreger, A.D., C. Chase, A. Sousa, P. Grappuso and J. Frader. 2005. "Changing the Nomenclature/Taxonomy for Intersex: A Scientific and Clinical Rationale". *Journal of Pediatric Endocrinology & Metabolism* 18 (8): 729–733.

Duro, P. 1988. "Copyists in the Louvre in the middle decades of the nineteenth century." *Gazette des Beaux Arts* 111: 249–254.

Ferentinos, S. 2019. "Ways of interpreting queer pasts". *The Public Historian* 41 (2): 19–43.

Foster, S.M. 2015. "Circulating agency: The V&A, Scotland, and the multiplication of plaster casts of 'Celtic Crosses'". *Journal of the History of Collecting* 27 (1): 73–96.

Frost, S. 2013. "Secret Histories: hidden histories of sex and sexuality". *Museums and Social Issues* 3 (1): 29–40.

Frost, S. 2021. "Interpreting LGBTQ histories at the British Museum". In *Museum Innovation: Building More Equitable, Relevant and Impactful Museums,* edited by E. Haitham and M. Forstrum, 123–135. London: Routledge.

Greaves, A. 2018. "Putting the 'T', the 'Q' and the 'I' into LGBTQI Classics: An example of museum-based learning". *CUCD Bulletin* 47: 1–6.

Gurian, E. H. 2005. "Threshold fear". In *Reclaiming Museum Space,* edited by S. McCleod, 204–214. London: Taylor & Francis.

Halperin, D. 1990. *One Hundred Years of Homosexuality: and other essays on Greek love.* London: Routledge.

Heimlich, J and J. Koke. 2013. "Gay and lesbian visitors and cultural institutions: Do the come? Do they care? A pilot study". *Museums and Social Issues* 3 (1): 93–104.

Holmes-Henderson, A. 2021. "Developing multiliteracies through classical mythology in British classrooms". In *Our Mythical Education: The Reception of Classical Myth Worldwide in Formal Education, 1900–2020,* edited by L. Maurice, 139–151. Warsaw: Warsaw University Press.

Holmes-Henderson, A. and K. Kelly. 2022. *Ancient Languages in Primary Schools in England: A Literature Review.* Department for Education. Accessed 17 November 2022. https://assets.publishing.service.gov.uk/government/uploads/system/uploads/attachment_data/file/1120024/Ancient_languages_in_primary_schools_in_England_-_A_Literature_Review.pdf.

Hooper-Greenhill, E. 2000. *Museums and the Interpretation of Visual Culture.* London: Routledge.

Knott, L, L. Jimenez, S. Rickard, J. Silvester, L. Stancliffe and S. Turner. 2020. "Museum Remix at the Museum of Classical Archaeology". *UCM Connecting Collections blog.* Accessed 16 September 2021. https://www.museums.cam.ac.uk/blog/2020/06/05/museum-remix-at-the-museum-of-classical-archaeology/.

Lovatt, H. 2011. "Sitting on the fence or breaking through the hedge? Risk taking, incentives and institutional barriers to outreach work among academics and students". In *Arts and Humanities Academics in Schools: Mapping the Pedagogical Interface*, edited by G. Baker and A. Fisher, 28–42. London: A&C Black.

Maguire, M. 2017. *Goddesses*. New Zealand: PaperGraphica.

Parkinson, R. 2013. *A Little Gay History: Desire and Diversity across the World*. London: British Museum Press.

Parry, R., R. Page and A. Moseley 2018. *Museums Thresholds: The Design and Media of Arrival*. London: Routledge.

Shoulder, J. and M. Small. 2020. "Greek Love and MuseumBums". *UCM Connecting Collections blog*. Accessed 16 September 2021. https://www.museums.cam.ac.uk/blog/2020/05/28/greek-love-and-museumbums/.

Siapkas, J. and L. Sjörgen 2014. *Displaying the Ideals of Antiquity: The Petrified Gaze*. London: Routledge.

Squire, M. 2018. "Introduction". In *The Classical Now*, edited by M. Squire, J. Cahill and R. Allen 2018, xii-xv. Milton Keynes: Elephant Publishing.

Squire, M., J. Cahill and R. Allen 2018. *The Classical Now*. Milton Keynes: Elephant Publishing.

Stafford, E. 2020. "Exhibiting Maguire's Herakles: A Dialogue between Old and New Worlds". In *The Modern Hercules*, edited by A. J.L. Blanshard and E. Stafford, 299–327. Leiden: Brill.

Stevens, T. 2018–2019. "The plaster cast collection of the Glasgow School of Art: History, Aura and Experience". *Journal of the Scottish Society for Art History* 23: 23–30.

Thornber, J. 2017. "Wanderings with a Camera with Cambridge Community Arts". *UCM Connecting Collections blog*. Accessed 9 September 2021. https://www.museums.cam.ac.uk/blog/2017/08/11/wanderings-with-a-camera-with-cambridge-community-arts/.

Thornber, J. 2018a. "Drink and Draw at the Museum of Classical Archaeology". *UCM Connecting Collections blog*. Accessed 9 September 2021. https://www.museums.cam.ac.uk/blog/2018/05/21/drink-and-draw-at-the-museum-of-classical-archaeology/.

Thornber, J. 2018b. "Amo, amas, amat... and so much more than that: The Minimus Primary Latin Project". *UCM Connecting Collections blog*. Accessed 11 November 2021. https://www.museums.cam.ac.uk/blog/2018/11/01/amo-amas-amat-and-so-much-more-than-that-the-minimus-primary-latin-project/.

Thornber, J. 2020. "Casting light on the ancient world: Education in the Museum of Classical Archaeology, Cambridge". In *Material Cultures in Public Engagement: Re-Inventing Public Archaeology within Museum Collections*, edited by A. Christophilopoulou, 133–144. Oxford: Oxbow.

Tseliou, M-A. 2013. *"Museums and Heteronormativity: Exploring the Effects of Inclusive Interpretative Strategies"*. Unpublished PhD thesis: University of Leicester.

Turner, S. 2020. "'Magical': an ongoing partnership with Cambridge Community Arts". *UCM Connecting Collections blog.* Accessed 9 September 2021. https://www.museums.cam.ac.uk/blog/2020/06/02/magical-an-ongoing-partnership-with-cambridge-community-arts/.

Turpin, J. 1983. "The South Kensington System and the Dublin Metropolitan School of Art 1877-1900". *Dublin Historical Record* 36 (2), 42–64.

Vout, C. 2015. *Following Hercules: The Story of Classical Art.* Cambridge: Fitzwilliam Museum.

Wade, R. 2018. *Domenico Brucciani and the Formatori of 19th-Century Britain.* London: Bloomsbury.

Whitehead, C. 2009. *Museums and the Construction of Disciplines: Art and Archaeology in Nineteenth-Century Britain.* London: Bloomsbury.

Winkler-Horaček, L. 2016. "Akademische Abguss-Sammlung en zwischen Tradition und Zukunft: Die Abguss-Sammlung Antiker Plastik der Freien Universität Berlin". In *Casting. Ein analoger Weg ins Zeitalter der Digitalisierung*, edited by C. Haak and M. Helfrich, Art Historicum. Accessed 9 September 2021. https://doi.org/10.11588/arthistoricum.536.

7 Contested Collections

Using 3D replicas to present new narratives of objects with contested histories

Emma Payne and Laura Gibson

Introduction

The Contested Collections project, funded by an Economic and Social Research Council Impact Acceleration Account (ESRC IAA) with King's College London, incorporates a set of learning materials and 3D object replicas to introduce learners aged 9–11 to aspects of art and material culture in the ancient world. Crucially, it also encourages them to learn about the increasingly urgent issue of decolonisation, a concept that we unpack during the project and address in this article. Each Collection contains six objects held by UK museums: the Parthenon sculptures, Lamassu, Benin Bronzes, Hoa Hakananai'a, Rosetta Stone and Gweagal shield. All of the objects are contested and have faced requests for repatriation because of their colonialist or imperialist histories. Rather than sidestepping the difficult, and sometimes violent circumstances surrounding acquisition, learners are encouraged to think carefully and critically about the various groups of people to whom these objects are important. The aim is both to develop learners' knowledge of different cultures and histories, and to start to give this generation of future leaders the language and skills to develop their own opinions and voices concerning how (and where) these objects might most appropriately be housed and understood, who should be responsible for making such decisions and how they relate to broader issues of colonialism and decolonisation.

Choosing a meaningful logo

Encapsulating the Contested Collections project is our logo (see Figure 7.1) designed by Hardeep Dhindsa, a PhD student in the Classics Department at King's College London, and one of our volunteer collaborators. The logo is based on one of the pieces of sculpture from

DOI: 10.4324/9781003181958-8

CONTESTED
COLLECTIONS

Figure 7.1 Contested Collections logo.
Source: © Hardeep Dhindsa for Contested Collections.

the Parthenon famously brought from Athens to Britain in the early nineteenth-century by Lord Elgin. One of the 92 sculpted metopes of the Parthenon, these architectural elements were positioned above the architrave of the temple and alternated with triglyphs (carved panels with three vertical channels) in the Doric style of classical architecture. Carved in Pentelic marble, this particular metope was originally positioned along the south side of the temple (South Metope XXXI), which depicted the battle between the legendary Greek people, the Lapiths and the part-human and part-horse mythical beasts, the centaurs.[1] No longer complete, the centaur is missing much of his right arm and part of his right hind leg, while the Lapith has lost much of his left arm and left foot.[2] Also absent is the coloured paint which once would have covered the surface of the panel.

The fragmentary nature of this panel, lacking its original surface finish, illustrates some of the difficulties faced by archaeologists today when researching the appearance of the Parthenon and its sculptures which were constructed in classical Athens, in the mid fifth-century BCE, under the auspices of the renowned ancient sculptor, Phidias. The incomplete sculpture hints at the turbulent history of this building which has left physical traces on its material structure. Over the course of its 2,500-year history, the temple has been struck by earthquake and fire, converted to a church and then a cathedral; following the surrender of Athens to the Ottoman Empire in 1456, the Parthenon was converted once again, this time to become a mosque, now within an Ottoman fortress, as the Acropolis housed the Turkish military commander. When the Venetians attacked the Ottomans in 1687, they scored a direct hit on the Parthenon, which was being used to store gunpowder. This attack ravaged many of the sculptures that were located on the long southern side of the building, particularly those like South Metope XXXI.[3]

The later years of the Ottoman occupation in Athens were marked by the campaigns of Choiseul-Gouffier and Elgin, respectively the French and British ambassadors to the Ottoman Empire around the turn of the nineteenth-century. Both men spent enormous amounts of time, energy and money on the study and recording of the ancient sculptures and structures of the Athenian Acropolis. Elgin in particular, however, would become notorious for removing many of these sculptures, both pulling them down from the building and digging up pieces buried following the 1687 explosion, and shipping them to Britain where they would later be bought by the government for the British Museum. Even at the time, Elgin's removal of the sculptures drew criticism from many quarters, and the validity and extent of the authorisation granted by his 'firman' from the Ottomans has also been questioned.[4]

We can see the physical impact of this turbulent history on South Metope XXXI. When developing this logo, we also wanted to reflect the Parthenon's contested history and felt that this was captured by the combative subject-matter of the sculpture, the struggle between Lapith and centaur. It is this contestation on which our project aims to shine a light for the benefit of primary school learners to assist them with navigating difficult histories through object handling and the development of targeted, but balanced, object narratives. The Parthenon sculptures, as arguably the most famously contested objects in Britain, formed the first lens through which this project was conceived.

Contesting colour

Each object in the Contested Collection has a short, illustrated, written narrative designed to provide an overview of its entire history, from creation to its present context (Figure 7.2). Accompanying learning materials include the physical 3D print (Figures 7.4a-c) and suggested classroom activities. The proposed activities incorporate both learning about the object in the context of its making and original culture and thinking about the different claims to ownership made in recent years. For the Parthenon, for example, activities include colouring to encourage learners to think about the original polychromy of the sculptures, as well as writing a letter to the British Museum to explain why they support or oppose returning the pieces to Greece. These kinds of authentic tasks are designed to foster deep approaches to learning (Entwistle

CONTESTED COLLECTION: PARTHENON SCULPTURES

STUDENT SHEET

Origin: Temple of the Parthenon, Athens, Greece

Current location: British Museum, London

What are the Parthenon Sculptures?

The Parthenon Sculptures are a group of ancient Greek marble sculptures, many of which are on display in the British Museum. They originally came from the Temple of the Parthenon on the Acropolis in Athens (above). The building was constructed between 447 and 438 BC. The majority of the Parthenon Sculptures in the British Museum are from the frieze of the Parthenon and are about 75m long, almost as long as Big Ben is tall! They depict people celebrating an ancient festival, gods and goddesses, and some myths. Originally the sculptures were brightly painted and some of the figures had metal fittings like helmets attached to them!

Figure 7.2 Excerpt from the Parthenon Sculptures object narrative.

and Ramsden 2015). As pedagogical experts Jan Meyer and Ray Land (2005) argue, complex and meaningful tasks allow students to think more like researchers and professionals and, significantly, have value that stretches far beyond the end of the programme (Boud 2000).

The whiteness of classical sculpture was historically drawn upon as evidence of its idealised perfection and was perpetuated by the spread of white plaster casts (Payne 2021, 167). Such an interpretation has been undermined by studies of polychromy demonstrating conclusively that the majority of classical sculpture was painted.[5] Nevertheless, the first objects to introduce learners to the classical world still tend to be the overwhelmingly white sculptures and casts filling museums and galleries. Hardeep Dhindsa's work seeks to add colour back into this narrative, as he did with the project's logo (Figure 7.1), providing a brightly coloured drawing of the Lapith and centaur, and reminding us both of ongoing studies into the polychromy of these works and of the broader impact of the attribution of 'whiteness' to these classical sculptures, which were sent around the world in the form of plaster casts to adorn colonial museums as examples of 'perfection'. Therefore, to expand learners' understanding of art and material culture within this broader colonial context, while inspired first by the Parthenon sculptures, the Contested Collection is not focused solely on the classical world but incorporates objects from a range of different time periods and places, all of which were impacted by histories of colonialism and Empire.

Shaping the Contested Collection

Following George Floyd's death in May 2020 and the ensuing Black Lives Matter protests, urgent questions arose surrounding societal and institutional racial inequity and the challenge of 'decolonisation'. British museums that hold colonial-era artefacts came under renewed scrutiny for their role in perpetuating colonial violence, with commentators likening these to Nazi-looted art (Bakare 2020; Hicks 2020a). The need for improved education in this area was underlined in the recent independent review of the Windrush scandal commissioned by the UK government, which identified a widespread lack of historical understanding about the UK's 'relationship with the rest of the world, including Britain's colonial history' (Williams 2020).

The Contested Collections project therefore seeks to provide school learners with the skills, language and confidence to engage in complex debates around decolonisation by providing a set of learning materials and 3D prints of objects whose ownership, acquisition and histories are contested, and which are currently held in UK museums. Six Contested Collections have now been created and will soon be sent to six UK primary schools, together with accompanying object narratives and teacher resources. The schools will be encouraged to keep the Collection so they can be reused for multiple lessons and for different classes. Distribution of the Contested Collections into schools was delayed by the COVID-19 pandemic; therefore, we will focus here on the first phases of the project.

One of our primary concerns when developing the project was to include as many diverse voices as possible. To that end, we recruited 12 volunteer student collaborators from King's College London. Interested students were asked to send us two short paragraphs: one about themselves and why they were interested in the project; the other briefly outlining a cultural heritage object with a contested history in which they were particularly interested or concerned. We received over 50 expressions of interest and in our selection of 12, we tried to include students who were interested in objects from a broad range of different cultures, across Africa, Asia, Europe, the Americas and Australia. A number of the students chose objects which resonated with their own family heritage. We selected seven undergraduate students, two taught postgraduate students and three research postgraduate students. To assist with the project, we also brought in

Dr Ikram Ghabriel, a researcher specializing in Egyptian archaeology and decolonisation in archaeology.

To ensure our learning materials were pitched at the appropriate level, we worked closely with educational partners, including Arlene Holmes-Henderson and Martin Spafford. Arlene Holmes-Henderson holds a doctorate in Classics Education and has worked on numerous international learning projects. Martin Spafford, as an associate of the Runnymede Trust, has extensive experience teaching History in secondary schools and has produced a range of activity-based learning programmes for primary school learners. Both The Latin Programme and The Iris Project also nominated school teachers to take part in our developmental workshops to generate and refine new written narratives dealing with the histories of the objects and suggested classroom activities.[6] Those involved with these initiatives have expertise in expanding access to knowledge of the classical world and its languages to learners in schools where there is no current provision. Through Contested Collections, we intend to build upon this expertise to develop learners' knowledge of different historical societies specifically through their art and material culture and to reinforce this knowledge by handling objects.

Workshop development phase

We designed the initial phase of the project around a programme of four workshops. At the first workshop, attended by the project leaders and student collaborators, we discussed how to define 'decolonisation' and explored the role 3D printed objects would play in the Collection. Following these discussions, at the second workshop, students each presented objects they thought would be good candidates for the Collection, including brief examinations of the contested aspects of their history and consideration of their suitability for 3D printing. After this workshop, students voted on a shortlist of eight objects for the Collection (Table 7.1); the students who presented the selected objects drafted short narratives about their histories, aimed at learners aged nine to 11.

In subsequent conversations with Dr Ghabriel, the students reflected that they were very pleased to be part of the project, and, for some, the workshops surpassed their expectations, while others wished for more discussion time during the sessions. One student was already active in repatriation discussions before joining the project, but the others felt they had learnt something new about decolonisation and repatriation through the workshops. Some mentioned that they now had a better awareness of the difficulties and limitations of 3D printing, and, in a non-pandemic situation, we would hope to engage the students more actively in this production phase of the project, rather than simply sharing the final products with them.

We were joined by our education partners in the final two workshops, who helped us to refine the object narratives and generate ideas for related learning activities.

Defining decolonisation

Since the term 'decolonisation' has been defined and deployed in so many different contexts, we made time during our first workshop to discuss how we understood this concept within the framework of the Contested Collections project. We offered students a number of prompts to begin thinking about this. They were not necessarily the best definitions or examples but we also wanted to show that interest in decolonisation is not new, that there is no single definition and yet there exists a plethora of individuals and institutions engaged in interpreting what decolonisation can mean. We included, for example, South African academics Dr Bongani Ndhlovu and Ayanda Nombila's 2020 interpretation of Z. K. Matthews' work as a way of reminding students that people in the Global South have been engaging with these ideas for decades.[7] Born in 1901, Z. K. Matthews was a prominent member of South Africa's African National Congress (ANC) party and a vital part of the anti-apartheid movement. For Z. K., decolonising African knowledge meant Africans creating new knowledge, transforming education curricula and a focus on African languages.

To highlight the ways institutions are grappling with this notion in the present day, we drew on various organisations' understandings of the term, including Chatham House's (2020) definition whereby:

> Decolonization takes many forms. In museums, it is often associated with custodianship and the returning of artefacts as well as the full accreditation of events – often violent – that brought historical items into Western collections. In schools and universities, it involves ensuring curricula accurately reflect a global conversation, while in the field of journalism and media, decolonization involves representation, diversity and appreciating cultural sensitivities.[8]

And, given that the Contested Collections focuses more immediately on artefacts, we offered a number of museum-specific interpretations, such as from Professor Dan Hicks' *The Brutish Museums* (2020b, 235–239), where he argues that:

> Grass-roots movements are beginning to connect questions of repatriation and fallism with those of restitution, questions of institutional racism with those of the uses of museums as mouthpieces for outdated ideas of social evolution, cultural difference and white supremacy, and the challenge of decolonising knowledge in universities and in society with anthropology museums as public spaces.

The students were given a few minutes to mull over these ideas and then each asked to give their own short definition of 'decolonisation' in a sentence or two. Based on these student responses, we drew together the following points as key to our understanding of what decolonisation would entail for this project:

- Recognizing the harm caused by colonialism.
- Acknowledging other cultures and perspectives.
- Decentring narratives.
- Shifting power.
- Restitution of land, objects, agency.

We aimed to address these points through the object narratives and learning activities by giving due weight to exploration of the making of the objects and the cultures responsible for them; by not shying away from violent events surrounding their acquisition by the UK; and by asking learners directly to try to think from different perspectives – for instance, those of visitors to UK museums and those from descendant communities and countries from which the objects were taken. Learners are asked to consider where it might now be best to keep these objects and who should make that decision, as shown in Figure 7.3.

One of the key impacts the project hopes to achieve is to equip learners with sensitivity to other cultures and to provide them with the necessary vocabulary and frameworks to contribute to future discussions.

Selecting and creating the 3D objects

One of the most exciting aspects of the project is the role played by 3D replica handling objects, bringing the learners a tangible connection to the material culture of different communities (see Figure 7.4a–c). The continued relevance of understanding historical cultures (including

118 *Emma Payne and Laura Gibson*

CONTESTED COLLECTION: GWEAGAL SHIELD

Who should own the Gweagal Shield now?

A great grandson of Cooman wants the shield back in Australia. He says it belongs to the Gweagal people and that the shield was violently stolen.

The British Museum does not want to return the shield. The Museum says that they studied the shield again and it is from Australia but is not Cooman's shield. The Gweagal people argue that the British Museum is studying the wrong **sources**. Other people say the shield is still Aboriginal Australian and must be returned anyway. It is probably the oldest Australian shield anywhere in the world.

THINKING POINT 3:

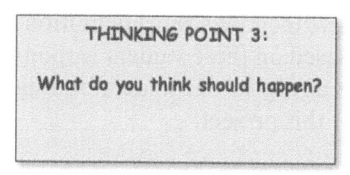

What do you think should happen?

Figure 7.3 Excerpt from the Gweagal Shield object narrative showing a student 'Thinking Point'.

those surviving to this day) is underlined by urgent debates surrounding the treatment of these contested objects. Appropriate production and use of such 3D objects, however, requires considerable care, as also discussed at our first workshop. We reviewed different methods of 3D printing with their various associated costs, strengths and weaknesses, and we also considered the different uses to which such objects might be put and the positives and negatives associated with each use (Table 7.1).

One of the biggest obstacles to full appreciation of museum objects, and therefore to understanding of ancient material culture, is that handling is rarely permitted. Handling museum objects is known to provide tangible therapeutic benefits, demonstrated in various studies in *Touch and Wellbeing* led by University College London (see for instance Thomson and Chatterjee 2016). Surrogate objects in the form of 3D prints can potentially provide a way to bridge this gap, especially when used for educational purposes. Such objects may be particularly useful for those with visual difficulties, enabling them to gain a better understanding of the original by handling a very close replica (Wilson et al. 2020).

The very act of object handling has been shown by data collected by University College London (UCL) to improve knowledge acquisition by 25–75 per cent.[9] This is of course a statistic we hope will prove contingent in this project, and which drove the inclusion of the 3D objects as a critical component. Interestingly for Contested Collections, some 3D printed objects have also been used for repatriation. One such example is the Conall Cael bell, which is an eighth century pilgrim bell from Donegal in Ireland. The original is kept in the British Museum but was recently loaned back to Donegal. After it was returned to the British Museum, a replica bell was commissioned to be used as part of the annual ceremony, which sees pilgrims walking across the causeway to the island monastery. A further case concerns the Igbo-Ukwu bronzes, which were found buried in Igbo, Nigeria, in the 1950s, and are dated to the ninth-century CE. Most are now in the National

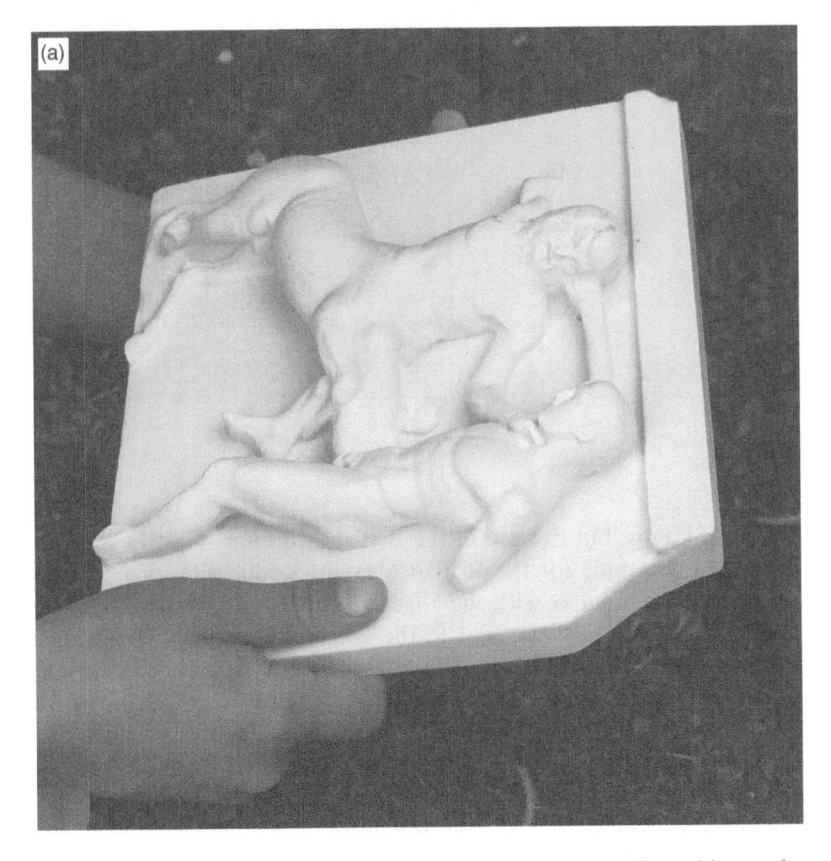

Figure 7.4 (a–c) Handling three of the Contested Collection objects: the metope from the Parthenon, a Benin Bronze plaque and the Hoa Hakananai'a. *(Continued)*

Figure 7.4 (Continued)

Museum Lagos, but five are in the British Museum. The 3D replicas of these were made for the British Museum's education programme and were very popular with the Nigerian community in Britain. As a result, some replicas were sent to the Igbo-Ukwu village where they were received emotionally, particularly by those who had been present during their excavation decades earlier.[10]

The concept of repatriation via replica raises a whole new set of issues and questions (see for example Salmond 2012; Boast and Enote 2013; Hollinger et al. 2013; Were 2014). There may be advantages, for instance, in insurance costs and potential usage: the creation of the replica Conall Cael bell means it can now be actively used, which would not be possible with the fragile original. However, significant issues persist surrounding the relative value ascribed to the original

Figure 7.4 (Continued)

versus the copy and the appropriateness of repatriation via replica, particularly for objects with religious or spiritual significance. The Acropolis Museum, for example, displays highly accurate plaster casts in place of those sections of the Parthenon sculptures housed at the British Museum. Although these casts may be very interesting and

Table 7.1 The eight shortlisted objects selected by the King's College London students

Parthenon sculptures	British Museum 1816,0610.15	Fifth-century BCE marble sculptures from the Parthenon, Athens. Taken by Elgin under the Ottoman Empire and brought to Britain in the early nineteenth century.
Lamassu	British Museum 1850,1228.2	Ninth-century BCE gypsum sculpture from Nimrud, ancient Assyria (modern Iraq). Excavated by Austen Henry Layard; permission to ship the sculpture (and its partner) to Britain granted by the Ottoman Empire.
Benin Bronzes	British Museum Af1898,0115.98	Sixteenth/seventeenth-century CE brass plaques made for the royal court of the Kingdom of Benin (southern Nigeria). Many of the plaques were forcibly taken by British soldiers in 1897, as Nigeria was colonised by Britain.
Hoa Hakananai'a	British Museum Oc1869,1005.1	Tenth/twelfth-century CE basalt sculpture from Rapa Nui (Easter Island). Excavated from a ceremonial house by British forces led by Richard Ashmore Powell and shipped to Britain.
Rosetta Stone	British Museum EA24	c. 196 BCE granodiorite stelae discovered by French soldier at Rashid (Rosetta), Egypt in CE 1799. The stele was sent to Britain the year after British forces defeated the French in Egypt in 1801.
Gweagal shield	British Museum Oc1978,Q.839	Eighteenth-century CE wooden shield from New South Wales, Australia. When Captain James Cook landed at Kamay (Botany Bay) in 1770, he allegedly shot at the Gweagal warrior, Cooman, who dropped his shield. Cook brought the shield back to Britain.
Asante Head	Wallace Collection OA1683	Eighteenth/nineteenth-century CE gold trophy head from the Ashanti Kingdom (modern-day Ghana). The head was forcibly taken by British soldiers during the Anglo-Ashanti war in 1873–1874. In Britain, it was sold to the jeweller, Garrard & Co, from whom Richard Wallace bought the head.

(Continued)

Table 7.1 The eight shortlisted objects selected by the King's College London students *(Continued)*

Koh-i-Noor diamond	Royal Collection RCIN 31703	A large cut diamond first recorded in the seventeenth century CE. It is known to have belonged to Shah Jahan, the emperor of the Mughal Empire, but subsequently changed owners many times. In 1843, it came into the possession of Duleep Singh, who inherited the throne of the Sikh Empire after his father was murdered. The diamond was taken by the British when they invaded Singh's land in 1849. It was given to Queen Victoria and incorporated into the Crown Jewels; it is now set within Queen Elizabeth The Queen Mother's Crown.

valuable in their own right, clearly, they do not have the same historical significance as the marble sculptures and they are not viewed as adequate replacements.[11]

Nevertheless, the goal of the Contested Collection is to spark debate surrounding issues such as repatriation, not to attempt to enact such a process. The primary role of the objects in this case is as educational instruments. These scaled-down representative objects allow learners to handle the artefacts, build a tangible connection with them and consequently begin dialogues about the objects' histories and questions of ownership. Rather like the Conall Cael bell, the use of replicas in this instance means that learners get the chance to touch objects when the original versions would be considered too vulnerable or too valuable.

When creating the replicas, they had necessarily to be scaled down. The Lamassu, for instance, is around 3.5 metres tall and the Hoa Hakananai'a around 2.5 metres tall. It is widely acknowledged, however, that for 3D replicas to be used most effectively they need to convey adequately the properties of the original objects (see for instance Wilson et al. 2017, 459–460; Wilson et al. 2018). Of course, it was impossible for us to create such large replicas, but we were careful to provide real-life indications of size within the object narratives; for instance, the British Museum has around 75 metres of Parthenon frieze 'almost as long as Big Ben is tall'. The replicas themselves are approximately 20 centimetres tall and to scale.

Features over which we had more control were surface quality and the weight of the objects. Giving the objects appropriate weight and ensuring high-quality surface finish should encourage learners to approach the objects with due care and respect, since they are handling pieces that hold great historical value and, in cases such as the Hoa Hakananai'a, religious significance. However, because we wanted to create objects that adequately reflected the originals, we made the decision to remove the golden Asante Head and the Koh-i-Noor diamond from the Collection. In spite of the difficulty faced when 3D imaging such reflective materials, the King's College London students had included these two artefacts in the final list of eight because they are such important examples of contested objects and derive from cultures understudied in UK schools. Ultimately, however, the material difficulties proved insurmountable within our budget and were compounded by the closure of museums during the COVID-19 pandemic since we had no access to photograph or scan the originals ourselves.

The lack of access to collections meant that the remaining six objects were worked up from existing, freely available 3D models and photographs. The 3D models and physical prints were created by the specialist staff at ThinkSee3D. Where 3D data was not available, models were digitally sculpted using photographs as a guide; photographs were also used to provide texture. Such an approach would not be appropriate for 3D models used for scientific research, but the results were nevertheless excellent and suitably accurate for scaled-down handling objects. The scaling of the objects meant not all details could be included, for instance, the scaling-down of the Lamassu was so significant that it was not possible to include its cuneiform inscriptions. However, fine detail was included as far as possible. For instance, the carving on the back of the Hoa Hakananai'a was replicated; the inscriptions on the Rosetta Stone were printed rather than carved due to the scale, but these are legible and it is clear that three different scripts are present.

One of the main problems with 3D printing is the lightweight plastic often employed, which does not sufficiently convey the properties of the material of the original and may appear cheap and flimsy; the importance of conveying such qualities is emphasised by Wilson et al. (2020, 14). 3D printing is now possible in a wider range of materials, using metal or gypsum powders, or even ceramics; however, such production can be very expensive. To solve these issues, for most of the Contested Collection objects, a single 3D print was produced, which was then moulded and cast in a material that would give a closer impression of the original both in appearance and in weight. This process of moulding and casting is adaptable and much cheaper than

3D printing; it also produces high-quality results. The replica Benin Bronze plaques, for example, were cast in polyurethane bulked with real bronze powder, while the replica Parthenon metopes were cast using Jesmonite (a gypsum-based powder in acrylic resin) mixed with marble powder. Where fine surface detail was required, which could not be modelled, as in the case of the Rosetta Stone, the outer shell of the object was 3D printed (in this case using a gypsum-based material) and then filled (with Jesmonite) to give additional weight.

Next phase

Once delivered, evaluation of this project will relate to the success of our approach in creating constructive debate about decolonisation; specifically, we will be assessing whether expanding access to 3D objects, and the ability to touch those objects, improves learning and stimulates debate in classroom contexts, as suggested by the UCL study. We will be assessing this outcome through teacher interviews and learner questionnaires. Given that this is a pilot project, our intention is to incorporate any suggested changes into a second iteration of the Contested Collection, both in terms of revising the objects we include and the learning materials that accompany them. We hope this improved version will be shared with a larger number of schools in the UK, ideally with support from the Department for Education. Based on other studies such as the 2019 Runnymede Trust and University of Liverpool's TIDE project, teaching about migration, belonging and empire is not only important for inclusion and representation but also equips young people with the vocabulary, skills and confidence to talk about these issues in meaningful ways, improving their overall sense of well-being (McIntosh et al. 2019). It is our hope that this project expands young people's involvement in arts, culture, heritage and museum education and also helps them develop as informed citizens.

Notes

1. For a concise introduction, see Jenkins (2006, 71–107).
2. https://www.britishmuseum.org/collection/object/G_1816-0610-15.
3. On the post-antique history of the Parthenon, see Ousterhout (2005, 293–330).
4. Elgin was most famously opposed by Lord Byron, but others like Edward Dodwell and Robert Smirke also wrote of their horror at seeing the sculptures pulled down (see Payne 2021, 46; 62).
5. Physical traces of colour have been confirmed both on the remains of the Parthenon standing on the Acropolis and on the sculptures in the British Museum. See Verri (2009) and Papakonstantinou-Ziotis (2012).

6 The Latin Programme works to improve literacy and to foster individuality, diversity and creativity, by delivering dynamic, rigorous and engaging Latin lessons to London state school pupils: https://www.thelatinprogramme.co.uk. The Iris Project is an educational charity aimed at bringing ancient languages and culture to inner city state schools and communities: http://irisproject.org.uk/index.php. Six copies of the Contested Collection will first be brought to state schools working with The Latin Programme or The Iris Project.
7 https://twitter.com/100_storyafrica/status/1327269137064800259.
8 https://www.chathamhouse.org/events/all/members-event/understanding-decolonization-21st-century.
9 https://www.ucl.ac.uk/teaching-learning/teaching-excellence-framework-tef/tef-2017/tef-2017-ucl-narrative-submission/learning-environment.
10 Both the cases of the Conall Cael bell and the Ugbo-Ukwu bronzes were facilitated by ThinkSee3D, who created the replicas (Personal communication with Steven Dey, May 2021).
11 There are some cases where a museum has retained the replica and returned the original, as for instance with the Killer Whale clan crest hat formerly housed at the Smithsonian Museum of Natural History and returned to the Tlingit community (Hollinger et al. 2013).

Reference List

Bakare, L. 2020. "Colonial Art in UK Museums Is Similar to Nazi-Looted Works, Says Charity Boss". *The Guardian*, 22 July. Accessed 12 May 2021. https://www.theguardian.com/world/2020/jul/22/colonial-art-in-uk-museums-is-similar-to-nazi-looted-works-says-charity-boss.

Boast, R. and J. Enote 2013. "Virtual Repatriation: It Is Neither Virtual nor Repatriation". In *Heritage in the Context of Globalization: Europe and the Americas*, edited by P. F. Biehl, 103–113. New York: Springer.

Boud, D. 2000. "Sustainable Assessment: Rethinking Assessment for the Learning Society." *Studies in Continuing Education* 22 (2): 151–167. Accessed 12 May 2021. https://doi.org/10.1080/713695728.

Entwistle, N. and P. Ramsden. 2015. *Understanding Student Learning*. Abingdon and New York: Routledge Revivals, Routledge.

Hicks, D. 2020a. "Will Europe's Museums Rise to the Challenge of Decolonisation?" *The Guardian*, 7 March. Accessed 12 May 2021. https://www.theguardian.com/world/commentisfree/2020/mar/07/europe-museums-decolonisation-africa-empire

Hicks, D. 2020b. *The Brutish Museums: The Benin Bronzes, Colonial Violence and Cultural Restitution*. London: Pluto Press.

Hollinger, R. E., E. John, H. Jacobs, L. Moran-Collins, C. Thorne, J. Zastrow, A. Metallo, G. Waibel and V. Rossi. 2013. "Tlingit-Smithsonian Collaborations with 3D Digitization of Cultural Objects." *Museum Anthropology Review* 7 (1–2): 201–253. Accessed 13 May 2021. https://scholarworks.iu.edu/journals/index.php/mar/article/view/2173/4567.

Jenkins, I. 2006. *Greek Architecture and Its Sculpture in the British Museum.* London: The British Museum Press.

McIntosh, K., J. Todd and N. Das. 2019. "Teaching Migration, Belonging, and Empire in Secondary Schools. TIDE and the Runnymede Trust". Accessed 12 May 2021. http://www.tideproject.uk/wp-content/uploads/2019/07/TIDE-Runnymede-Teaching-Migration_Summary_July-2019.pdf.

Meyer, J. H. F. and R. Land. 2005. "Threshold Concepts and Troublesome Knowledge (2): Epistemological Considerations and a Conceptual Framework for Teaching and Learning". *Higher Education* 49 (3): 373–388. Accessed 12 May 2021. https://doi.org/10.1007/s10734-004-6779-5.

Ousterhout, R. 2005. "'Bestride the very peak of heaven': The Parthenon after antiquity". In *The Parthenon: From Antiquity to the Present*, edited by J. Neils, 293–330. Cambridge: Cambridge University Press.

Papakonstantinou-Ziotis, E. 2012. "Surface conservation". In *Acropolis Restored*, edited by C. Bouras, M. Ioannidou and I. Jenkins, 57–64. London: The British Museum Press.

Payne, E. M. 2021. *Casting the Parthenon Sculptures from the Eighteenth Century to the Digital Age.* London and New York: Bloomsbury.

Salmond, A. 2012. "Digital Subjects, Cultural Objects: Special Issue Introduction". *Journal of Material Culture* 17 (3): 211–228.

Thomson, L. J. and H. J. Chatterjee. 2016. "Wellbeing with Objects: Evaluating a museum object-handling intervention for older adults in health care settings". *Journal of Applied Gerontology* 35 (3): 349–362. Accessed 11 May 2021. http://dx.doi.org/10.1177/0733464814558267.

Verri, G. 2009. "The spatially resolved characterisation of Egyptian blue, Han blue and Han purple by photo-induced luminescence digital imaging". *Analytical and Bioanalytical Chemistry* 394: 1011–1021.

Were, G. 2014. "Digital Heritage, Knowledge Networks, and Source Communities: Understanding Digital Objects in a Melanesian Society". *Museum Anthropology* 37 (2): 133–143.

Williams, W. 2020. "Windrush Lessons Learned Review". *Home Office* 140. Accessed 11 May 2021. https://www.gov.uk/government/publications/windrush-lessons-learned-review.

Wilson, P. F., S. Griffiths, E. Williams, M. P. Smith and M. A. Williams. 2020. "Designing 3-D prints for blind and partially sighted audiences in museums: Exploring the needs of those living with sight loss". *Visitor Studies* 23 (10): 1–21.

Wilson, P. F., J. Stott, M. Warnett, A. Attridge, M. P. Smith and M. A. Williams. 2017. "Evaluation of touchable 3D-printed replicas in museums". *Curator* 60 (4): 445–465. https://doi.org/10.1111/cura.12244.

Wilson, P. F., J. Stott, M. Warnett, A. Attridge, M. P. Smith and M. A. Williams. 2018. "Museum visitor preference for the physical properties of 3D printed replicas". *Journal of Cultural Heritage* 32: 176–185.

Index

A-Level 1, 3, 4, 5, 31, 39, 40–41, 73, 75, 88
access 1–5, 25, 30–32, 42–43, 61, 62, 73, 79, 85, 91, 93, 99, 115, 124, 125
Achaemenids 79
acquiescence bias 26
Additional Language, English as (EAL) 4, 16–17, 24, 27, 42–52, 56, 72
Africa 56, 58, 59, 67, 114; languages of 116
African National Congress (ANC) 116
agency 87, 117
Alexander the Great 56
Alexandria 63
Alma-Tadema, Lawrence 93
Ancient History (subject) 1, 3–4, 5, 31, 39, 56, 72–88
animation 25–26
Aphrodite 94, 97
Apollo Belvedere 96, 101
archaeology 25, 38, 60, 93, 111, 115
architecture 31, 35, 111
Aristogeiton 96
art, contemporary 92–94, 98
Art History 25, 96, 110, 115
Ashanti Kingdom 122
Ashurbanipal II 78, 79
Ashurnasirpal 78, 79
assessment 25, 27, 79–80, 81; baseline 38
Assyrians 79, 85
Athena 94
Athens 31, 96, 101, 111, 112, 122; Acropolis of 111–112, 121, 125n5
Australia 114, 122

Babylon 75, 78, 79
BAME people 3, 56–69, 75, 79, 85, 88n4
Bassae, temple of Apollo at 97
Beard, Mary 90
Belfast, Northern Ireland 21
Berlin, Germany 93
Benin Bronzes 6, 110, 119, 122, 125
bilingualism 46
Birmingham 21, 23, 88n5
Black Lives Matter (BLM) 57–58, 114
Blackpool 4, 30–32, 33, 35, 36, 37, 38, 39, 40, 41n4
British Museum 25, 101, 112, 119–120, 121–122
Bronze Age Collapse 78
Buckinghamshire 1, 56

Cambridge, Cambridgeshire 1, 2, 8, 19, 21, 23, 60; Museum of Classical Archaeology (MOCA) 90–104
Cambridge Latin Course see also Latin courses
Cambyses II, king of Persia 78, 79
casts, plaster 90–96, 98, 100–102, 113, 121, 124–125
Caracalla, emperor 98
Choiseul-Gouffier, Auguste de 112
Cicero 2
citizenship 33, 68, 125
civilisation, idea of 56, 77–78
Classical Civilisation (subject) 1, 4, 31, 39, 73, 86
Classics For All Project 3, 31–32, 39–40

Index 129

Classics in Communities Project 4, 8, 10, 21–22, 25, 26
clubs, Latin 99–100
colonialism 6, 110, 113–114, 117 *see also* decolonization
Conall Cael bell 119, 120, 123, 126n10
Contested Collections Project 6, 110–125
Cook, James 122
cookery 11
Cooman (Gweagal warrior) 122
Covid-19 pandemic 35, 38, 114, 124
creativity 11, 44, 94, 126n6
crime 30
critical thinking 50, 102
curriculum, absent 76, 87
Cyrus the Great, king of Persia 75, 78, 79

Darius I, king of Persia 74, 78, 79
decolonization 6, 57, 63, 69, 110, 114–115, 125; definitions of 116–117
deprivation, socio-economic 18, 30, 37, 42; Multiple Deprivation, Index of (IMD) 72
Derby, Derbyshire 4, 42
disability 3, 15, 27n3, 62
disadvantage, socio-economic 4, 13, 19, 24, 33, 34, 36
discrimination 2, 43, 45, 59
diversity 5, 11, 43, 56, 58, 59, 62–63, 67, 69, 73, 85, 88, 101, 116, 126n6
drama 11, 33
'Drink and Draw' events 5, 92–93

Egypt 78, 115, 122
Elgin, Lord 111–112, 122, 125n4
'Elgin Marbles' *see* Parthenon sculptures
elitism 2, 11, 42, 56, 60, 61, 83
empire 2, 79, 84, 114, 125 *see also* colonialism; imperialism
ethnic minorities *see* BAME people
etymology 15, 34, 35, 37, 38, 45, 49, 51
exhibitions 92, 93–95

fallism 117
feminism 94

festivals 99
Fife 18
Floyd, George 114
fluency, oral 4
Free School Meals (FSM), pupils eligible for 4, 14–15, 18, 27, 34, 72

GCSE 5, 36, 44, 56, 73–74, 75–76, 77, 79, 88n3
gender 33, 59, 62, 96, 97
Ghana 122
Glasgow 18, 21, 23, 104n9
grammar 8, 10–11, 15, 17, 18–19, 33, 34, 36–37, 40, 47, 57, 99
Greek, Ancient 1, 4, 8, 9, 10, 18, 21, 22, 23, 24–26, 27, 31, 35, 36, 39–40, 48, 49, 61; alphabet 18, 22, 26
Gweagal shield 110, 118, 122

Hadrian's Wall 59
Hannibal 56
Harmodius 96
Hera 94
Hercules 96
Hermaphroditus 98, 105n16
Herodotus 79
History, Ancient *see* Ancient History (subject)
Hittites 78
Hoa Hakananai'a 110, 119, 122, 123, 124
Homer 18, 31; *Iliad* 18, 51 (*see also* Trojan War); *Odyssey* 5, 18, 45–46, 47–9, 50–51, 52

Igbo-Ukwu bronzes 119–120
imperialism 57, 86, 101, 110; *see also* colonialism; empire
inclusivity 3, 57, 58, 60, 61, 69, 72–88, 95
individuality 11
Iris Project 8, 9, 18–21, 115
Islam *see* Muslims
Italian 38, 43

Key Stages: KS1 41n3; KS2 8, 24–26, 31, 36, 41n3; KS3 5, 36, 37, 42, 43, 56, 57, 72, 75; KS4 44, 56, 73, 75; KS5 56, 73

kingship 79
Koh-i-Noor Diamond 123, 124

Lamassu 110, 122, 123, 124
languages, modern foreign (MFL) 33, 36, 38
Latin courses: *Cambridge Latin Course* 5, 40, 57, 61, 62–63, 65; *Minimus Primary Latin Project* 6, 24, 33, 34, 37–38, 40, 98–100; *Suburani* 5, 40, 57, 58, 65
Latin Programme, The 9–18, 26, 115, 126n6
Lego 38
Leighton, Frederick 93
LGBTQIA+ communities 3, 95–98
literacy 4, 8, 9, 10–11, 12–15, 16, 17, 18, 19, 20, 24–25, 27, 32, 34, 40, 48, 74, 85, 126n6
Lollius Urbicus, Quintus 59

Manchester 18
Matthews, Z. K. 116
Middle East, ancient 5, 72, 75–76, 77–80, 81–85, 86–88
morphemes *see* morphology
morphology 15, 27, 38, 48–49, 51, 52
Mughal Empire 123
museums 1, 4, 5–6, 18, 25–26, 90–104, 110, 112, 113, 114, 116–117, 118–120, 121, 122, 123, 124, 125
music (songs) 11, 33, 100
Muslims 5, 76–77, 79–88
mythology, Classical 4, 42–52, 105n18

Nabopolassar 79
nation-building 79
National Curriculum 9, 43
Nebuchadnezzar II 78, 79
Needs, Special Educational (SEN) 4, 15–16, 24, 27, 41n2
Nigeria 119, 120, 122
Nimrud, Iraq 122
Nottingham, Nottinghamshire 105n17

objects, Classical 6, 92, 94, 95, 96, 99, 100, 102, 104, 110–125; handling of 112, 115, 117, 118, 119, 123, 124; object-based learning 100

Ofsted 18
oracy 4, 33, 38
orthography 27
Ottoman Empire 111–112, 122
Ovid 19
Oxford, University of 1, 2, 5, 8, 9, 18, 19, 21, 23

Pakistan 76, 82
Parthenon sculptures 6, 101, 110–111, 112–113, 119, 121, 122, 123, 125
Pericles 2
Persians 31, 56, 66–67, 75, 76, 77, 78
Phidias 111
philosophy 3, 73, 100
photography 94, 124
plays, Latin 36
policy, educational 2, 6, 8, 77
polychromy 101, 112, 113
poverty 30
Powell, Richard Ashmore 122
printing, 3D 6, 110–125
Professional Development, Continuing (CPD) 31, 33–34, 35, 36, 38, 39
progress, educational 8, 9, 11–12, 13–17, 37, 38, 46
Pupil Premium 34, 37, 39, 56

racism 62; institutional 117
Rapa Nui (Easter Island) 122
reading 4, 9, 10, 11, 14–15, 19–20, 25, 32, 33, 34, 41n3, 43, 47–49, 51, 57, 61; aloud 5, 46–47, 52; reciprocal 5, 49–50, 52
Reading, Berkshire 18, 105n17
Referral Units, Pupil (PRUs) 1, 4, 32, 33, 34–35, 40, 41n2
refugees 4, 42, 45
repatriation 6, 110, 115, 117, 119, 120, 121, 123
roots *see* etymology
restitution 6, 117
Roma-Slovak community 43
Roman Republic 31
Romani language 43, 44
Romanian 43
Rosetta Stone 110, 122, 124–125

Index 131

SATs 20, 33, 37, 41n3
schools: primary 1, 6, 8, 9, 14, 15, 18, 19, 21–22, 26, 27, 31, 32, 33, 36, 38, 39, 99, 112, 114–115; private (independent) 1, 3, 31, 35, 39; secondary 1, 4, 9, 21, 32, 33, 42, 44, 56, 72, 77, 115; state-maintained 1, 2–3, 4, 10, 18, 31, 34, 39, 88, 99, 126n6
Sea Peoples 78
Shah Jahan 123
Shakespeare, William 45, 51
Sikh Empire 123
Singh, Duleep 123
slavery 57, 59, 61, 63, 68, 74
Slovak language 43, 51
South Africa 116
stereotyping 35, 62
Swansea, Wales 18, 105n17
syncretism, religious 68
syntax 27, 43, 46

teaching, non-specialist 4, 9, 10, 21, 33, 35, 40
textbooks 5, 11, 18, 22, 56–69
Tiglath Pileser II 78, 79
training, teacher 4, 19, 21, 35, 69
translation 4, 39, 42

Travellers, Gypsy Roma (GRT) 43
Trojan War 45, 59–60

Ugarit 78
Ur 78
Urdu 43

Venetians 111
Victoria, queen of the United Kingdom 123
Victoria and Albert Museum 97
vocabulary development 4, 10, 15, 18, 31, 32–33, 34, 35, 36–37, 39–40, 44, 46, 47, 48, 49, 50, 51–52, 99, 117, 125

Wallace Collection 122
Walsall, West Midlands 5, 72
warfare 79, 86
white supremacy 59, 117
white-washing 2
Windrush Scandal 114
workshops 9, 21, 22–23, 24, 35, 115, 116, 118
writing 5, 9, 10, 11, 14–15, 18, 19–20, 35, 51; creative 45, 52

Yaba 79
York, Yorkshire 59